SpringerBriefs in Computer Science

For further volumes:
http://www.springer.com/series/10028

Gerardo I. Simari • Simon D. Parsons

Markov Decision Processes and the Belief-Desire-Intention Model

Bridging the Gap for Autonomous Agents

 Springer

Gerardo I. Simari
Department of Computer Science
University of Oxford
United Kingdom
gerardo.simari@cs.ox.ac.uk

Simon D. Parsons
Department of Computer
and Information Science
Brooklyn College
City University of New York
New York
USA
parsons@sci.brooklyn.cuny.edu

ISSN 2191-5768   e-ISSN 2191-5776
ISBN 978-1-4614-1471-1   e-ISBN 978-1-4614-1472-8
DOI 10.1007/978-1-4614-1472-8
Springer New York Dordrecht Heidelberg London

Library of Congress Control Number: 2011937480

Printed on acid-free paper

Springer is part of Springer Science+Business Media (www.springer.com)

Acknowledgements

This work was possible due to generous support from *Comisión de Investigaciones Científicas de la Provincia de Buenos Aires* (Argentina) granted to Gerardo Simari during his time at *Laboratorio de Investigación y Desarrollo en Inteligencia Artificial* (LIDIA) at *Universidad Nacional del Sur* (Bahía Blanca, Argentina).

The authors are grateful to Martijn Schut for sharing code with them, and to Agent Oriented Software for a license for JACK that allowed them to use that code. Finally, the authors would also like to thank the anonymous reviewers who provided valuable feedback on earlier versions of this work; their comments and suggestions helped improve this manuscript.

Contents

Chapter 1
Introduction

Autonomy is arguably the most important feature of an intelligent agent since it dictates that the agent can make decisions on its own, without any outside help. In simple environments this is not difficult to achieve: a simple search through the possible actions and states will yield the best thing to do in every case, and the associated computation will be tractable. However, the situation changes drastically in complex environments. Agents in these conditions will often need to act under uncertainty; this means that they will not always be sure about what state they are in, nor will they be sure about the outcomes of their actions.

The problem of establishing the best mechanism by which an agent can make decisions has been widely studied, and several approaches have been formulated to tackle this problem in a wide variety of ways. In this work, we will focus on two models that have been proposed as ways to attack it. The first is the *Belief-Desire-Intention* (BDI) model, which will be discussed in Section 2.1; this model falls into the class of *descriptive* approaches—approaches that are based on analyzing the way that people or animals make decisions. The second model, the *Markov Decision Process* (MDPs)[1], belongs to the class of *prescriptive* approaches—approaches that attempt to identify the optimal decision, that are typically based around Decision Theory (Raiffa., 1968). The necessary background for this model will be covered in Section 2.2.

Since the BDI model, and implementations thereof, have been widely used by agent developers, it is interesting to ask about the quality of the decisions that the model makes. It seems natural that this will depend upon the exact nature of the task; this was experimentally validated by Kinny and Georgeff (Kinny and Georgeff, 1991). In particular, Kinny and Georgeff showed that the performance of an agent depended upon the speed with which its environment changed, the amount of information the agent has at its disposal, and the likelihood of its actions having

---

[1] The more general *Partially Observable Markov Decision Process* (POMDP) model could also have been adopted. However, for the purposes of this work we will consider mainly the fully observable case, with some exceptions (cf. Section 4.4); this is mainly due to the fact that MDPs are simpler, and it was natural to begin with the simpler case. Extending all of our results to partially observable domains is an interesting prospect for future work.

their intended effect. Another of Kinny and Georgeff's findings was that the performance of the agent depended upon how often, broadly speaking, it considered whether it had made the right decision (its *commitment strategy* in the language of the BDI model). Following up on this, Schut and Wooldridge (Schut, 2002; Schut and Wooldridge, 2000, 2001) considered a range of models for making this meta-level decision about whether the last decision was still a good one, even using an MDP model (Schut et al, 2001) to optimize it. This topic is called *intention reconsideration*, and has been discussed in some detail in the literature. See, for example (Bratman et al, 1991; Bratman, 1987; Kinny and Georgeff, 1991; Wooldridge and Parsons, 1999; Schut and Wooldridge, 2000; Parsons et al, 1999; Schut et al, 2001) and, more recently, (Fagundes et al, 2009; Tan et al, 2010).

Problem statement. All of the work discussed above has only been able to compare different commitment strategies with one another using a metric of how well the agent performs on the task rather than with any notion of what the optimum performance is. All that we know is that, as a heuristic approach, the BDI model is likely to be sub-optimal. We just do not know *how* sub-optimal. The trade-off, the reason we may be prepared to accept this sub-optimality, is that the BDI model is in the general case much more tractable than prescriptive approaches like MDPs. The main goal of this work is to investigate the characteristics of this trade-off. As we shall see, MDPs can be intractable even for rather small problems when we do not resort to approximations; however, we will show experimentally that even quite rudimentary approximations to the solutions to these intractable problems outperform the BDI model.

Main Contributions. This work builds on the work of Schut and Wooldridge (Schut et al, 2001), which deals with trying to understand the relationship between the BDI model and MDPs. We do this in two different ways:

- First, in Chapter 3 we give an empirical comparison of the two models. In particular, we examine how good a solution the BDI model produces in comparison with MDPs on the testbed used first by Kinny and Georgeff (Kinny and Georgeff, 1991) and then by Schut and Wooldridge. It turns out that in order to apply MDPs on the testbed, we need to resort to approximations; we report these as well as the results of the comparison with BDI.
- Second, in Chapter 4 we give a formal analysis of the relationship between the two models. In particular, we establish relationships between the main components of each model, and provide a mapping between intentions on the BDI side and policies on the MDP side.

Note: The empirical comparison of models is not meant to be one between state-of-the-art implementations or approximation techniques; this would be a major undertaking on its own). Instead, the spirit of our approach is to investigate the basic relationships and tradeoffs between the two models. We will explain our approach in more detail in Chapter 3.

Chapter 2
Preliminary Concepts

In this chapter, we will include introductory concepts to the two models that will be used in the rest of this work, the BDI architecture and Markov Decision Processes.

2.1 The BDI Model

Belief-Desire-Intention (BDI) models are a family of models that were inspired by the philosophical tradition of understanding *practical reasoning*, and were first proposed by (Bratman, 1987; Bratman et al, 1991). This type of reasoning can be described as the process of deciding what actions to perform in order to reach a goal. Practical reasoning involves two important processes: decide *what* goals to try and reach, and *how* to reach them. The first process is known as *deliberation*, and the output of deliberation is a set of *intentions*, things that the deliberator will commit resources to try to bring about. The second process is considered to be a process of *means-ends* reasoning, that is working out a sequence of actions that will achieve the intentions. Bratman includes the following definition in (Bratman, 1990):

> Practical reasoning is a matter of weighing conflicting considerations for and against competing actions, where the relevant considerations are provided by what the agent desires/values/cares about and what the agent believes.

Practical reasoning, as described, seems to be a straightforward process, at least for humans, who can often perform it many times in a brief moment and without much effort. However the concept translates into a series of non-trivial complications when viewed from the perspective of an arbitrary autonomous agent. First of all, deliberation and means-ends reasoning are computational processes, which means that they are subject to the resource bounds (such as space and time) available to the system. These bounds set a limit to the amount of computation that an agent will be able to perform in a given time span. These limits have two important implications (Wooldridge, 2000):

- Computation is a valuable resource for agents situated in real-time (either with soft or hard bounds) environments. The efficient use of computational resources will play an important role in the agent's ability to select adequate actions. In other words, the agent's performance is tied to the *control* of its reasoning (Bratman et al, 1991; Russell and Wefald, 1992; Russell et al, 1993); and
- Agents cannot deliberate indefinitely. It is clear that the process must halt at some point in order to be useful. It may well be the case that, after stopping, the commitments selected will not be the best ones; had the agent spent more time, it might have settled for other commitments.

Note that practical reasoning is different from *theoretical reasoning*, which is directed towards beliefs, whereas practical reasoning is directed towards *action*. Proving theorems in first order logic representing an agent's beliefs is theoretical reasoning because it only affects the formulas in the belief set; deciding whether to throw a ball or not is practical reasoning because it affects the actions that the agent will perform.

The BDI model is an interesting architecture to study because it involves the following elements (Wooldridge, 2000):

- It is founded upon a well-known and highly respected theory of rational action in humans;
- It has been implemented and successfully used in a number of complex fielded applications; and
- The theory has been rigorously formalized in a family of BDI logics.

These points have played a major role in the success of the BDI model, which is now one of the most studied models in the field and has also been used as the basis for a number of implementations (Fisher, 1997; Georgeff and Ingrand, 1989; Howden et al, 2001; Huber, 1999; Jo and Arnold, 2002; Machado and Bordini, 2002).

One of the classic problems in the design of practical reasoning agents is how to obtain a good *balance* between deliberation, means-ends reasoning, and action (since an agent that does not eventually act is not of any practical use). Specifically, it seems clear that an agent must, at some point, drop some of its intentions (for any of several possible reasons). It follows, then, that it is worthwhile for the agent to stop and *reconsider* its intentions. But reconsideration has its costs, both in time and computational resources. This situation presents an interesting tradeoff:

- An agent that does not stop to reconsider often enough will continue trying to reach *outdated intentions*.
- If the agent *constantly* reconsiders its intentions, it might spend too much time deliberating and will therefore not get anything done. In this case, it is possible that the agent will never reach its intentions.

This is essentially the dilemma of balancing *proactive* (goal directed) and *reactive* (event directed) behavior. This situation described was examined by David Kinny and Michael Georgeff, in a number of experiments performed with an implementation of the BDI model called *dMARS*. They investigated how *bold* agents (those that never stop to reconsider) and *cautious* agents (those that constantly reconsider) behave in a variety of different environments. The most important parameter in these experiments was the *rate of change* of the world, γ. Kinny and Georgeff's key results were (Kinny and Georgeff, 1991):

- If γ is low (*i.e.*, the environment does not change rapidly), then bold agents work well with respect to cautious ones. This is because cautious agents waste their time reconsidering their commitments while bold agents work to reach their goals.
- If γ is high (*i.e.*, the environment changes frequently), then cautious agents tend to perform better than bold ones, because they can recognize when their intentions are no longer valid, and they can take advantage of new opportunities when they arise.

The result is that different types of environments require different types of decision strategies. In static environments, proactive behavior is adequate. In more dynamic environments, the ability to react to changes by modifying intentions becomes more important. Therefore, there is no "best way" to resolve the balance mentioned. Each application must be *tuned* to its environment, and therefore the best balance depends on the application. The best way to resolve this conflict may therefore be to implement an adaptation mechanism, with which agents recognize how often they must stop to reconsider their intentions.

The practical reasoning process can be broken down into a number of basic components, as discussed, for example, in (Wooldridge, 1999). One view of these components is:

- A set of current *beliefs*, B, which represents the information that the agent currently maintains both about its internal state and its environment.
- A set of *desires*, D, which represents the agent's possible courses of action.
- A set of *intentions*, I, which represents the agent's current focus, *i.e.*, those states to which it is committed to bring about.
- A *belief revision* function, *brf*, which takes a perceptual input and the agent's current beliefs and, based on this, determines the new set of beliefs.
- An *option generation* function, *options*, which determines the possible alternatives available to the agent based on the current beliefs about the environment and its current *intentions*. This function represents one part of the agent's deliberation component, as described above. It maps a set of beliefs and a set of intentions into a set of *desires*.
- A *filter* function, *filter* which represents the rest of the agent's *deliberation* component. This determines a consistent set of intentions based on its current beliefs, desires, and intentions.
- A *planning* function, *plan* which implements means-ends reasoning as described above. This function maps the current set of beliefs and intentions to sequence of actions Π.

Without considering refinements such as commitment strategies (Cohen and Levesque, 1990; Kinny and Georgeff, 1991), these components work together as in Figure 2.1.

```
1.    B := B_0;
2.    I := I_0;
3.    while true do
4.          get next percept ρ;
5.          B := brf(B,ρ);
6.          D := options(B,I);
7.          I := filter(B,D,I);
8.          Π := plan(B,I);
9.          execute(Π)
10.   end while
```

Fig. 2.1 A high-level description of the main processes in the BDI model.

(See (Wooldridge, 2000) for a series of more detailed refinements of this description). We can think of this machinery as being captured by a tuple[1]:

$$\langle S, A, Bel, Des, Int, brf, M, \rangle$$

The BDI literature often assigns different meanings to the term *intention* (for instance, it is often used both as presented above and to denote a linear plan built with the objective of reaching a certain goal). In this work, we will use the term *intention* to denote a state that an agent has committed to bring about, and use the term *intention-plan* (*i*-plan) to denote a sequence of actions built to reach a specific state, or, in other words, to achieve a specific intention. Since the precise sequence of actions selected will vary depending on what state the agent was in when it deliberated, an *i*-plan will depend on both the state that the agent is in, and the intention that it wishes to achieve — an agent will, in general, create different *i*-plans to achieve the same intention from different initial states, and will, in general, create different *i*-plans to achieve different intentions from the same initial state. Finally, an important point is that any set of intentions adopted by a single agent must be *consistent*, *i.e.*, there cannot exist conflicts between any pair in the set.

2.2 Markov Decision Processes

We will now describe a model useful for sequential decision making, called the *Markov Decision Process* model. In this work we assume that agents using this type of model have perfect sensors so that they always know *exactly* what state they are in, even though there is uncertainty about the effect of their actions. However, as we will see, the agent need not retain any information about the history of its past actions in order to make optimal decisions.

---

[1] This formulation is similar to some characterizations in the literature; for instance, see (Meneguzzi et al, 2004)

The problem here is, then, to find the best way to behave given a complete and correct model of the environment (and of course, a goal). The same problem has been addressed in AI as planning problems, but the consideration of stochastic domains forces us to depart from the traditional model and compute solutions in the form of *policies* instead of action sequences (plans) (Schoppers, 1987). A policy is a complete mapping from states to actions; once a policy is calculated from the transition model and the utility function (see below), it is trivial to decide what to do. The function that tells the agent what to do is represented explicitly by the policy: it describes a simple reflex agent. The problem of calculating an *optimal* policy in an *accessible, stochastic* environment with a known transition model is called a *Markov Decision Problem* (MDP). In decision problems, the *Markov property* holds if the transition probabilities from any given state depend only on the state and not on the previous history.

A Markov Decision Process can be defined, for example as in (Littman, 1996), as a tuple:

$$M = \langle S, A, T, R, \beta \rangle$$

where:

- S is a finite set of *states* of the environment. A state represents "the way the world currently exists". It is assumed that every detail necessary for deciding what to do is summarized in the state of the world.

  This set can become *very* large in a complex environment, as we will see later.
- A is a finite set of *actions*. This set contains every possible action that can be taken by the agent. Some actions cannot be performed in some states (for example, go forward while facing a wall); in these cases it is assumed that the action has no effect.
- A *state transition function*:

$$T : S \times A \mapsto f(S)$$

  This gives, for each state and action performed by the agent, a probability distribution over states. In other words, $T(s, a, s')$ is the probability of ending in state s', given that the agent started in state s and performs action a. The distribution will, in general, assign zero probability to some states, states that cannot be reached from s.

  To distinguish the set of states that may be reached by a given action from a given state, we write $a(s)$ to denote the set of states for which there is a non-zero probability of reaching after executing action a in state s, that is every state s' for which $T(s, a, s')$ is non-zero.
- A *reward function*:

$$R : S \mapsto \Re$$

  which gives the immediate reward gained by the agent for being in a particular state. It is also helpful to state the reward function in terms of state/action combinations

$$R_E : S \times A \to \Re$$

the subscript E serving to remind us that in this case the function returns the *expected* reward.

- $0 < \beta < 1$ is a *discount factor*, which is used in order to give higher values to rewards that are received earlier.

It is possible to extend the model in order to consider *infinite* state and action spaces. These models, commonly referred to as *continuous* models, will not be considered here.

The function T represents the transition to a new environment state that is produced as the result of the agent executing a particular action in a given state. In the MDP model, such transitions are considered to be *non-deterministic*. The impact of the in terms of finding a solution to an MDP is that since the result of executing an action cannot always be determined beforehand, we have to compute the weighted average of all the possible outcomes of that action (the expected value) in order to determine which action to take—this is exactly the reason that R_E can only compute the expected reward.

As a result, the solution to an MDP is not a sequence of actions but a *policy* π, where:

$$\pi : S \mapsto A$$

That is a policy specifies the action that should be selected for every possible state that the agent might find itself in. Now, any mapping from states to actions is a policy—it is not necessarily a good policy. A good policy is one that leads to a good level of reward, and the optimal policy for an MDP is the policy that gives the best possible expected reward for that MDP.

It should be noted that these transition probabilities do not explicitly consider the occurrence of *exogenous events*. Such events are considered to be those that, just like actions, cause stochastic transitions among states, but are not controlled by the agent. Exogenous events include the 'natural evolution' of the environment (such as passage of time), as well as actions performed by other agents occupying the same environment. This type of model has been called an *implicit event* model because the effect of exogenous events are implicitly considered by the transition probabilities associated with actions. On the other hand, an *explicit event model* considers transitions between states that are explicitly determined by the agent's actions *and* certain exogenous events, and which can occur with a given probability.

The rewards received by the agent define the objectives or the tasks that it must carry out and, therefore, their computation should be considered out of the reach of the agent's direct manipulation. The design of rewards is a crucial aspect that must be considered when defining a problem based on MDPs. Although it is not always considered so, many researchers deem this to be the most difficult point to establish in these systems (Mataríc, 1994; Errecalde, 2003; Regan and Boutilier, 2010).

Some general guidelines are useful in the design of rewards. Because agents under this model maximize their expected rewards, the idea is to establish rewards in such a way that when the agent does this, it behaves as desired. The common approach towards this is to define significant rewards only when terminal (objective) states are reached, and provide comparatively equal rewards in all other states. We will see an example of this type of reward definition in the MDP solution to the TILEWORLD in Chapter 3. There is no consensus on the advantages or disadvantages to defining significant rewards in intermediate states. Some researchers claim that the definition of significant rewards only in terminal states clearly denotes *what* should be accomplished, and not *how* it should be done. Others, however, state that the definition of intermediate states can have a significant impact on the acceleration of computing an optimal solution.

Chapter 3
An Empirical Comparison of Models

In this chapter we summarize our empirical evaluation of the BDI and MDP models. In turn we discuss the testbed that was used, the experimental setup, and the results of the experiments.

3.1 The TILEWORLD Domain

The TILEWORLD testbed (Pollack and Ringuette, 1990) is a grid environment occupied by agents, tiles, holes, and obstacles. The agent's objective is to score as many points as possible by filling up holes, which can be done by pushing the tiles into them. The agent can move in any direction (even diagonally); the only restriction is that the obstacles must be avoided. This environment is *dynamic*, so holes may appear and disappear randomly in accordance to a series of world parameters, which can be varied by the experimenter.

Because this environment, though simple to describe, is too complex for most experiments, we adopted the simplified testbed used in (Kinny and Georgeff, 1991) and (Schut and Wooldridge, 2000). Indeed, Martijn Schut kindly gave us a copy of his code to use in our work. The simplifications to the model are that (1) tiles are omitted, so an agent can score points simply by moving to a hole, (2) agents have perfect, zero-cost knowledge of the state of the world, and (3) in the case of the BDI model, agents build correct and complete plans for visiting a single hole (that is, they do not plan tours for visiting more than one hole). Though simplistic, this domain is useful in the evaluation of the effectiveness of situated agents. One of its main advantages is that it can be easily scaled up to provide computationally difficult and intractable problems.

Tractability and the TileWorld Domain

As we described in Chapter 2, in an MDP the world is modeled by taking into account *every* possible action in *every* possible state. For the simplified TILEWORLD, this means that for a world of size n (that is, an $n \times n$ grid) there is a set of

8 actions, n^2 possible positions for the agent, and 2^{n^2} possible configurations of holes. This last expression is obtained by considering that every position in the grid may contain a hole or not. A *state* in this world consists of a pair (P,H), where $P = (i,j), 0 \leq i,j \leq n-1$, and H represents a given configuration of holes on the grid. Therefore, the total number of states in this case is $n^2 2^{n^2}$; the fact that the number of distinct states for $n = 6$ is almost two and a half *trillion* shows the magnitude of this combinatorial explosion. Therefore, without resorting to state abstraction techniques and/or approximations, the MDP model requires an intractable amount of resources (both time and space) even for a very small TILEWORLD; the problem lies in the computation of an optimal policy using a method that enumerates every state (as the basic approaches to solution do). The limit for the tractability of this kind of direct calculation seems to be at $n = 4$, or $n = 5$ for a computer with reasonable resources. Direct calculation is, however, by no means necessary. There are a host of modern techniques that have been proposed for solving MDPs that are much more efficient than direct calculation. There have been many advances on this front (we refer the reader to our discussion of such techniques in Chapter 5); unfortunately, *no single technique* has been proven to date to be powerful enough to tackle the scalability issues that come up in general applications of MDPs (Geffner, 2010).

A Note Regarding Our Experimental Setup

Due to the reasons mentioned above, evaluating state-of-the-art approximation techniques for MDPs is outside the scope of our work; instead, we adopt the approach of comparing the performance of simple approximation techniques with equally simple implementations of the BDI model, with the objective of eliciting results that highlight how each model responds to variations in key parameters, as discussed in detail below.

As we will explain next, our simple approximation techniques will be based on the fact that the "explosion" in the number of states depends largely on the amount of holes that can be present at a given moment in the TileWorld; this gives us a means of approximating the solution by pretending that there are fewer holes than there really are. This is not a provably good approximation but, as we will see, it does not matter in general if the approximation is not perfect, as our heuristic-based MDP solvers outperform the BDI agent in nearly every case.

3.2 Obtaining Basic Approximate Solutions

In this section we describe some approaches that we have examined as a way to approximate the MDP for intractable sizes of the TILEWORLD. We believe that these are interesting not only because of their role in our experiments, but also because similar approaches may be useable in other applications of MDPs.

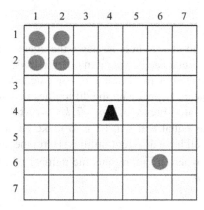

Fig. 3.1 An example TILEWORLD configuration

3.2.1 Reducing State Information

One possible way of keeping the computation of policies within acceptable bounds is to consider a *reduced state space*; this kind of techniques have been widely applied in the literature, as we will discuss in Chapter 5. This means that the agent will no longer have complete information regarding the current state of the world, *i.e.*, the current state will be *hashed* into one of the states in the reduced space. Of course, this will generally mean that the agent will no longer be able to select the optimal action in each step because there will always be information which the agent ignores and is necessary in order to make optimal choices. Therefore, the only way to obtain optimal policies under this model is to consider a degenerate hash, which contains all of the states in the environment. The action taken by the agent will therefore be optimal with respect to the reduced state space, and sub-optimal with respect to the full state-space in general. Nevertheless, if the hashing is a good one, the action will approximate the optimal action for the full state space. This hashing can be done in a variety of ways, trading-off between number of states and optimality. The following sections describe these proposals.

The Closest Hole

The agent is only aware of the closest hole. Even though it is simple, this strategy cannot ensure good results because an agent will not be able, for example, to decide between two closest holes as in Figure 3.1 ($n = 7$). Here, even though (2,2) and (6,6) are both the closest to the agent, (2,2) is the best option because it is close to a group of holes. This behavior is captured by Value Iteration (position (2,2) will have a greater utility than (6,6)), but will be ignored by the closest hole approach. In this case, the advantage is that the number of states is only n^4, which is much smaller than the full state space.

The k Closest Holes

As a generalization of the closest hole strategy, the agent can keep track of the k closest holes. The parameter k can be varied in order to trade efficiency against cost: $k = 1$ yields the previous approach, while $k = n^2$ is the general case discussed above. This generalization is meant to deal with the difficulties that arise for $k = 1$ but still suffers from cases like that in Figure 3.2 ($n = 7$, $k = 4$) where the agent will regard the four closest holes as equal and will have to make an arbitrary choice among them, even though they all have different utilities. Here, the number of states grows to $n^2 \sum_{i=1}^{k} C_i^{n^2} \leq n^2 2^{n^2}$, where C_k^n represents the number of combinations of size k taken from a set of size n.

Local Density

As an attempt to deal with the problems that arise from the previous strategy, the agent can keep track of the k closest holes along with additional information regarding the *local density* (in terms of holes) of the area in which the hole lies. This information can be used to make the right decision in cases like that of Figure 3.2.

The local density for a given position (i, j) that contains a hole can be calculated as the sum of the *influence* of every other hole in the world, where the influence is a value obtained as the product of the hole's reward and the inverse of the distance that lies between it and (i, j). More formally, the *density* of position (i, j) is

$$D_{i,j} = \sum_{(s,t) \in H, \ (s,t) \neq (i,j)} R'_{s,t} \frac{1}{Dist_{(i,j),(s,t)}}$$

where H is a set of ordered pairs containing the location of every hole in the grid, R' is the *reward function* on states, and $Dist_{(i,j),(s,t)}$ is the distance separating (i, j) from (s,t). In this approach, the number of states is the same as in the previous section because the size of the hashed state space has not changed, only the way the hashing is done. The calculation of the density information yields an additional cost. The distance between holes and the reward function on states can be calculated in $O(1)$, so the complete density information for *one* state can be obtained in $O(n^2)$.

3.2.2 Using Optimal Sub-solutions

When reducing state information we are pretending the problem is simpler than it is without changing its size. Alternatively, we can pretend the problem is smaller than it really is, making use of one or more solutions to the biggest version of the problem that we can compute.

One approach to doing this uses four 4×4 grids to make up a new 7×7 grid, which we refer to as the *moving window*. This can be done by putting the four

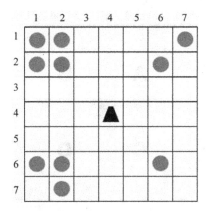

Fig. 3.2 Another example TILEWORLD configuration

grids together so they overlap one row; we will call these sub-grids A, B, C, and D (see Figure 3.3). This 7×7 grid is called a "moving window" because it follows the agent's moves, representing the limit of its perception. The agent occupies the center (*i.e.*, the SE corner of A, the SW corner of B, the NE corner of C, and the NW corner of D), and it will only be aware of the holes that fall inside this window. For example, if the agent is in the center of the grid, then it has full accessibility; now, if it moves North one position, it will not be able to see the holes to the far South.

Now, a new policy is built using the solved 4×4 sub-grids. For each state, the agent will have four possibly different suggestions (one for each 4×4), given by the policies:

$$\pi_i(s) = \arg\max_a \sum_t T_i(s,a,t)U_i(t)$$

where $i = A, B, C, D$, T_i is the state transition function for grid i, and U_i is the utility function on states for grid i. The best action is then the one that has the highest expected utility:

$$\pi^*(s) = \pi_i(s)$$

for some i such that $\pi_i(s) = t_i$, where $U_i(t_i) = u_i$ and there is no u_j such that $\pi_j(s) = t_j$, $U_j(t_j) = u_j$, and $u_j > u_i$.

The computational cost of this approach is not significantly greater than the cost of solving an MDP for a TILEWORLD of size 4×4. Because the policy is built from the policy for a 4×4, the only difference lies in execution time, where the hashing and the selection of the best action among the four suggested take place. The hashing can be done in $O(n^2)$ because each position must be tested to see if it falls inside the moving window; the execution time of both operations are clearly in $O(1)$.

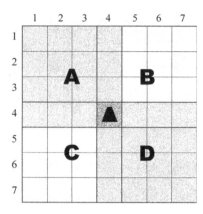

Fig. 3.3 The moving window

3.3 Experimental Results

We now present the results obtained after carrying out experimental investigation into the approximations described above; due to reasons of space, we present the most relevant results here, and refer the reader to (Simari, 2004) for the complete set of results.

We started from the experimental framework developed by Schut (Schut, 2002), using his implementation of the TILEWORLD and the adaptive BDI (Schut et al, 2001) model in JACK Intelligent Agents (Busetta et al, 1999)[1], and writing our own MDP solver. We then ran the BDI model and a selection of the MDP approximations (k closest holes for $k = 1, 2, 3$—each with and without the local density information—and the moving window) for a range of different values of dynamism, determinism, and accessibility. The empirical comparison will consist in the analysis of the *effectiveness* of three models: (1) *Adaptive* BDI, (2) MDP: *moving window approximation*, and (3) MDP: *reduced state space approximation*.

Effectiveness is a measure of how well the agent performs in the environment, and is calculated as the ratio between the number of holes it reached during the run and how many actually appeared. It must be noted that it could very well be the case that it is *impossible* to reach every hole during a run, even if the agent is theoretically optimal. This is because holes disappear after some time, and the agent might not be able to reach it before a given hole disappears when, for example, dynamism has a high value; therefore, effectiveness values are useful in comparing two models, but it should be kept in mind that they are not always on a 0 to 100% scale. It should also be noted that the measure of effectiveness has the desirable property of being independent from the computer on which the experiments are actually run; because it only considers how well the agent did in its choice of actions, how long the run actually takes is of no interest here. However, offline computation costs must

---

[1] http://www.agent-software.com/

Parameter	Value
World Dimension	7
Hole life expectancy	[240, 960]
Hole gestation time	[60, 240]
Dynamism	(1, 200)
Accessibility	(1, 7)
Determinism	(0, 100)
Number of time steps	25,000
Number of runs	30
Planning cost (BDI)	0, 2, or 4
Number of hashed holes (MDP Reduced)	1, 2, or 3
Use of Density information (MDP Reduced)	Yes or No

Table 3.1 Experimental parameters

not be disregarded, for they are the motivation for formulating the approximations described above.

In the following, the models will be compared in single-parameter variation experiments for:

- *Dynamism:* This parameter indicates how "fast" the agent acts with respect to the world. It is implemented as how many *steps* are executed by the world for every step the agent executes.
- *Determinism:* Indicates the probability of success for each action taken by the agent.
- *Accessibility:* The number of spaces the agent can "see" around itself.

Furthermore, models (1) and (3) have parameters of their own which will be varied in order to see how effectiveness is affected. In Adaptive BDI, *planning cost* (how many steps the agent must "invest" in building a plan), which will take the values 0, 2, or 4, and, in MDP: Reduced State Space, the number of holes in the hash will take the values 1, 2, or 3. This approach also includes the possibility of using "density information". At first, it was assumed that this information would make the agent more effective, but we will see that the results indicate otherwise. The maximum number of holes that can be considered in the hash is three because four holes yields a space of 231,525 states, which, in our implementation, is a larger number of states than can be considered. The number of states jumps considerably after four, and three holes offers good performance. Of course, the optimal performance can in principle only be obtained with 49 hashed holes (actually, no hash at all), but this is out of reach as stated above. During the experiments it was observed that no more than four or five holes appear at once (given the parameters used by Schut, see Table 3.1), which explains why only considering three holes is enough to provide good performance.

The experiments were carried out along the the lines of those described in (Schut and Wooldridge, 2000), where the authors compare the effectiveness of cautious, bold, and adaptive BDI agents. There are three parameters that we vary, and we only vary one of the parameters at a time. The values of the other two parameters are fixed as below:

- When we vary *Dynamism*, we set Accessibility to 7 and Determinism to 100.
- When we vary *Accessibility*, we set Dynamism to 1 and Determinism to 100.
- When we vary *Determinism*, we set Accessibility to 7 and Dynamism to 40. Dynamism assumes this value because of the reduced size of the environment. If it were set to 1, the agent would be able to reach virtually every hole by mere chance.

Because we carry out the experiments in a smaller TILEWORLD than the one used in (Schut and Wooldridge, 2000), we consider Dynamism values between 1 and 240 (instead of values between 1 and 80 as in (Schut and Wooldridge, 2000)). Since higher values of dynamism mean that more time steps go by between an agent's actions, higher dynamism seems appropriate for a smaller world. We also ran all the simulations for 25,000 time steps (instead of 15,000 as in (Schut and Wooldridge, 2000)).

In Table 3.1, we include the rest of the details of the experiments. In this table, $[x,y]$ denotes a uniform distribution of integer values between x and y, and (x,y) denotes the range of integer values from x to y. The number of runs was set to 30 because it was empirically determined that this value is large enough to minimize experimental error, that is, the standard deviation stabilizes after this value with respect to the number of time steps in each run.

3.3.1 Results for Dynamism

The results for varying Dynamism are shown in Figures 3.4 and 3.5. The general shapes of the curves in this analysis show that as the world becomes more dynamic, that is the holes appear and disappear with greater frequency, the effectiveness of the agent falls. This is to be expected, because after a certain point many of the holes tend to disappear before the agent can reach them. Using the BDI approach the agent periodically has to replan. When this happens the agent pauses for a certain number of time steps. These are the values of p that generate the three different curves.

Figure 3.4 summarizes the performance of each of the MDP approximations. It is clear that at lower values of Dynamism the Reduced State Space model outperforms the Moving Window, and that while considering 3 holes in this model yields the best results, there is little difference between the approaches at higher values of dynamism. It can be observed that the Moving Window agent is limited to an effectiveness of about 0.75; this is because its accessibility is inherently limited. Consider what would happen to the agent if it were to travel to a corner in order to fill a hole. Because its perception is limited to the window, it would only be able to see a little over one quarter of the environment. Now, until a hole appears within this space and "draws" the agent out of the corner, it will remain there, unable to perceive the holes that are appearing and disappearing in the rest of the world. This

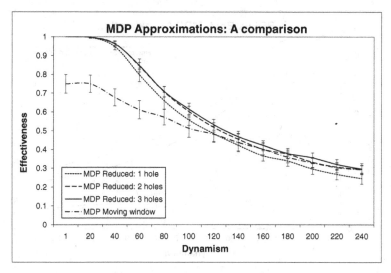

Fig. 3.4 A comparison among the different MDP approaches. The full line represents the reduced state space approach with three holes; the dashed line represents this approach with two holes, and the dotted line represents the approach with one hole. Finally, the dashed and dotted line that lies below the others represents the moving window approach. Error bars show one standard deviation above and below the mean.

can be somewhat relieved by implementing a simple random walk, which makes the agent walk around randomly when it does not perceive any holes. An implementation of this technique yielded better results, but are not included here for clarity of the presentation—they can be found in (Simari, 2004).

Figure 3.5 makes a comparison between the best performing MDP approximation and Schut's BDI model. This shows that the MDP model outperforms the BDI model over most values of Dynamism even when the BDI model does not have to spend any time replanning. So, even an approximation to the optimal model is better than the heuristic approach for a 7×7 TILEWORLD.

As a final note, we observed in the complete set of results (Simari, 2004) that the curves for the Reduced State Space MDP with and without density information allows us to conclude that this technique seems to detract from the performance of the model. The same trend was observed for all the approximations, and also for the rest of the single-parameter variations.

3.3.2 Results for Determinism

As in the analysis for Dynamism, we present two comparative graphs in order to analyze the empirical data we have gathered. Figure 3.6 shows a comparison among the MDP approximations we have considered. Even though the curves are very similar, once again we can see that the Reduced State Space approach with a hash of

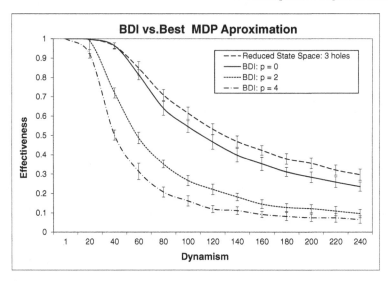

Fig. 3.5 A comparison among the best approximation to MDP and BDI with different planning costs. The dashed line represents the reduced state space approach to MDP with three holes (which was proven the best approximation in Figure 3.4). The full line represents BDI with planning cost 0; the dotted line represents BDI with planning cost 2, while the dashed and dotted line represents BDI with planning cost 4. Error bars show one standard deviation above and below the mean.

three holes outperforms the rest, followed closely by the hash with two holes. However the differences for values of Determinism below around 30 are negligible. We can see that the general results are expected, because they show that the agent's effectiveness will become better as its actions become more reliable. As before, we can observe the inherent limitation of the Moving Window model, as we discussed in the analysis of the results for Dynamism.

Figure 3.7 compares the Reduced State agent with the BDI agent with a range of planning costs. As with Dynamism, the approximated MDP solution outperforms the BDI agent for most values of Determinism, even when this agent has no planning cost. When the BDI agent takes time to plan (as, of course, it would have to if this were not a simulation), the MDP agent does significantly better.

3.3.3 Results for Accessibility

Once again, we present two comparative graphs in order to analyze how the variation of Accessibility impacts on effectiveness. Figure 3.8 shows a comparison among the MDP approximations. The three curves that are very close together represent the Reduced State Space agent, and the fourth corresponds to the Moving Window. From this graph we can gather that the number of holes considered in the hash does not greatly affect the performance of the agent when Accessibility is varied, because

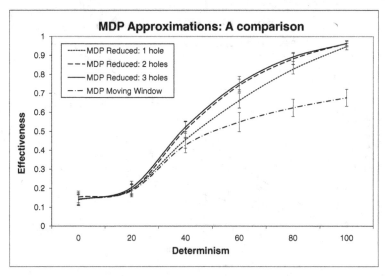

Fig. 3.6 A comparison among the different MDP approaches. The solid line represents the reduced state space approach with three holes; the dashed line represents this approach with two holes, and the dotted line represents the approach with one hole. Finally, the dashed and dotted line that lies below the others represents the moving window approach. Error bars show one standard deviation above and below the mean.

the curves are very close together, and the differences among them surely correspond to experimental fluctuations; we can be sure of this because both the curves and their standard deviations are very close together, and because the three hole approximation includes one *and* two holes. The Moving Window can once again be seen to be limited to an effectiveness of 75%, as we have seen in the analyses for both Dynamism and Determinism. We therefore select the Reduced State Space agent with three holes hashed as the predominant strategy. This irrelevance of number of hashed holes is due to the fact that the experiments took place in a 7×7 TILEWORLD, which is too small to make a difference in this parameter.

Figure 3.9 compares the MDP approximation with BDI. Once again, we can see that the curves are very close together, and cannot be distinguished from one another. We can also conclude from this that the MDP approximation is at least as good as the BDI model, and that the little difference among the curves is surely due to the fact that the experiments took place in a small environment.

3.3.4 A Larger Environment

As we saw in the previous sections, the performance of the BDI agent was consistently inferior to that of the different approximations to the MDP model. This result is not entirely surprising; after all, we are comparing a heuristic model against

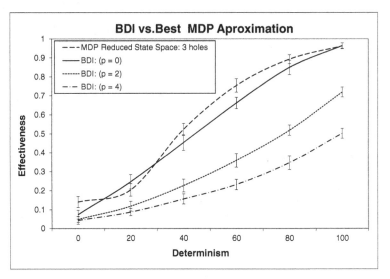

Fig. 3.7 A comparison among the best approximation to MDP and BDI with different planning costs. The dashed line represents the reduced state space approach to MDP with three holes (which proved to be the best approximation in Figure 3.6). The solid line represents BDI with planning cost 0; the dotted line represents BDI with planning cost 2, while the dashed and dotted line represents BDI with planning cost 4. Error bars show one standard deviation above and below the mean.

decision-theoretic optimality. However, as we will see next, the strength of prescriptive approaches lies in their capacity to 'cover' the state space in such a way as to conserve the ability to make approximately optimal decisions. In the 7×7 TILE-WORLD, we saw that the approximations used to make such decisions were overall better than those taken by the BDI agent. However, as we will see in this section, this situation is reversed as the size of the world becomes larger. In this section, we will describe how the agents from the previous experiments were adapted in order to inhabit a 20×20 TILEWORLD, and present graphs of their performance. Here, the results correspond to experiments carried out exactly as before, except that we concentrate on the variation of Dynamism. This is done both for clarity in the exposition and because Dynamism was clearly the most influential parameter studied in the previous sections.

The agents in this case are based on the same models as in the previous experiments, except that they were adapted to occupy larger worlds. This is where the heuristic approach embodied by the BDI model pays off. Because it is not trying to be exact, the BDI agent is able to see every square in the grid—the model scales with no problems. However, this is not true for the MDP agent. Constrained to be an exact model, the largest grid we can solve exactly for the MDP agent is the same 4×4 as before. As a result, the best we can do in this case is to implement the MDP agent as a 7×7 "moving window" (with the 7×7 made up of four overlapping 4×4 grids), thus limiting it to being able to see just 3 cells in all directions. (An

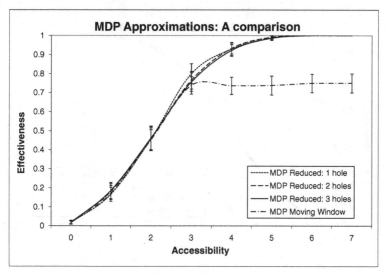

Fig. 3.8 A comparison among the different MDP approaches. The solid line represents the reduced state space approach with three holes; the dashed line represents this approach with two holes, and the dotted line represents the approach with one hole. Finally, the dashed and dotted line that lies below the others represents the moving window approach.

alternative would be to implement this moving window as a hash in the same way we did above.)

Figure 3.10 shows a summary of the results for the 20×20 TILEWORLD. We have selected the BDI planning cost 2 curve as a representative of the heuristic model, and for the MDP model we used the "moving window" based on the 4 overlapping 4×4 grids and the 3 hole reduced state space approximations. As the figure clearly shows, the BDI model now outperforms these MDP approximations. For low values of Dynamism, the BDI model is far superior and is never worse than the MDP approximations across the whole range of dynamism. As dynamism reaches extreme values, the effectiveness of the agents becomes close; this is due to the on-line planning cost that the BDI agent must pay and the fact that the holes are now disappearing before the agent can reach them. Finally, we note that the two MDP approximations are almost equivalent in this case. This is due to the fact that the differences in their implementations have little impact in a large environment.

3.4 Conclusions: Limitations and Significance of the Empirical Evaluation

There are two main conclusions we can draw from the analysis of our results. The first is that the MDP approach—effectively giving an agent a complete conditional plan—outperforms (or at least does as well as) the BDI approach in a 7×7 world

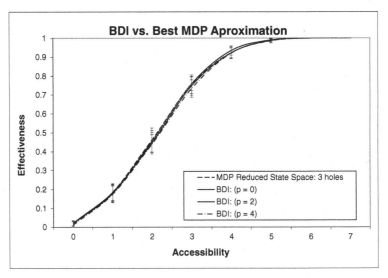

Fig. 3.9 A comparison among the best approximation to MDP and BDI with different planning costs. The dashed line represents the reduced state space approach to MDP with three holes (which was proven the best approximation in Figure 3.8). The solid line represents BDI with planning cost 0; the dotted line represents BDI with planning cost 2, while the dashed and dotted line represents BDI with planning cost 4.

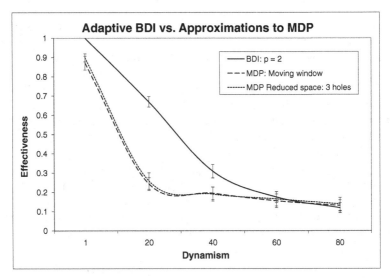

Fig. 3.10 Final comparison of models for a 20×20 environment.

even if the agent has a full set of linear plans that it switches between (which is the case we model when $p = 0$). While not surprising *per se*, since we are comparing a heuristic approach with decision-theoretic optimality, it is interesting that even an *approximation* to the MDP solution (and not a very sophisticated one) succeeds in this way.

Looking at the results from another angle, it seems that the approximations we have given for the MDP TILEWORLD model work reasonably well, since they can outperform a BDI model with an optimal mechanism for switching between plans (Schut et al, 2001) in a 7×7 world. While these approximations admittedly suffer from the limitation of being domain dependent as they stand, we believe that the same idea can be useful in other domains as a way of extending whatever maximum size of a problem can be solved by other approaches. This holds since rather than identifying efficient computational approaches to find the solution to a problem of a given size, they use the solution to a problem of a given size to approximate the solution to a larger problem.

Another important thing to note here is that the 20×20 TILEWORLD is larger than anything that can be solved by even the most powerful exact and approximate techniques for solving MDPs. We believe that this shows that the BDI model has a place in the armory of every agent designer since it makes it possible to build agents that perform better than those based on an optimal but insoluble, and thus necessarily badly approximated, model. Even existing approximations for solving MDPs will fail before some large problems that are soluble using the BDI model (Geffner, 2010).

Limitations of our approach. In summary, the main limitation of our empirical evaluation lies in the fact that state-of-the-art implementations of both models are not tested. As mentioned above, the main reason for doing this lies in the fact that our goal was not to evaluate specific techniques, but rather to investigate the fundamental ways in which both models react when key parameters are varied in order to obtain some insight regarding the tradeoffs that come with the adoption of each model.

Significance. Our results can be seen to be significant for various reasons: a thorough variation of parameters was investigated, and multiple runs were evaluated in each case in order to minimize experimental error; the TileWorld domain is a fairly general testbed that abstracts many scenarios of interest; and, finally. the approximation techniques are not *ad hoc* in the sense that they are based on solutions to smaller problem instances instead of identifying problem-specific points that can be leveraged.

In the next chapter, we will consider the problem of investigating the relationship between both models from a theoretical point of view.

Chapter 4
A Theoretical Comparison of Models

We have seen in the previous chapter that Markov Decision Processes can be considered an "ideal" approach to the implementation of intelligent agents. Even though assigning utilities to states and probabilities to transitions between states might be regarded as a questionable way to solve the problem of preference, there are many situations in which this is acceptable. Once we have accepted that the problem is correctly formulated in terms of the probabilities of actions having particular effects, and certain states having higher rewards than others, the MDP solution algorithms yield MEU-optimal policies. By this we mean mappings of states into actions that tell the agent what to do in *each* state, based on the probable outcomes of *every* possible action.

It is the nature of its solutions, and how they are computed, that render MDPs unusable when the size of the domain becomes more complex. In the empirical analysis of Chapter 3, we saw that complete solutions are only feasible for TILE-WORLDS of up to 4×4, and that for a 7×7 TILEWORLD it is necessary to resort to simplifying representations. This is where the BDI model steps in as a potential solution to these tractability problems; because of its heuristic nature, it does not necessarily promise optimal performance. Abstracting away from the deliberation and means-ends reasoning components of the model — which can be implemented in a variety of ways — it is the *i*-plans (the sequences of actions that achieve intentions from specific initial states), that are at the center of the BDI model. It is the *i*-plans that dictate how the agent will behave. Therefore, the relationship between these models that we present will be based on:

1. *From policies to i-plans*: Given a policy that is, in some way, the *solution* to a fully specified Markov Decision Problem, how can we obtain *i-plans* that a BDI agent can use to govern its behavior?
2. *From i-plans to policies*: Given a fully specified BDI agent, how can we obtain a *policy* that an MDP-based agent can use to control its actions?

4.1 Preliminary Mappings

In this section we will briefly discuss how actions, states, and transition functions corresponding to BDI and MDP agent functions can be mapped into each other, as introduced in (Schut et al, 2001). After establishing these preliminary mappings, we will define what exactly we consider to be an intention and i-plan in our model, and how such intentions and i-plans are related to the basic BDI model as discussed in Chapter 2. We will also argue how intentions and plans in general are related to the state space of an MDP.

As we have seen in Chapter 2, an MDP agent is defined by a state space, a set of actions, a reward function, and a state transition function which depends on the current state and the action performed; in the following, we will use S_{MKV}, A_{MKV}, R, and T_{MKV} to refer to these components, respectively. In contrast, a BDI agent is composed of a set of states (where each state is composed of a triple (B,D,I), of current beliefs, desires, and intentions, respectively), a set of actions, *internal* components (a belief revision function, an options generation function or means-ends reasoning component, and a *filter* function or deliberation component), and a state transition function that depends on the current state and the action performed; we will henceforth use S_{BDI}, A_{BDI}, and T_{BDI} to refer to the state space, the set of actions, and the transition functions for a BDI agent, respectively. Furthermore, because we are assuming that both agents occupy the same environment, it is clear that $A_{\mathrm{BDI}} \equiv A_{\mathrm{MKV}}$ and $T_{\mathrm{BDI}} \equiv T_{\mathrm{MKV}}$.

The last mapping that we consider here is between the state spaces of both models. The environment can either be fully or partially observable; in either case, we are assuming that the environment state is a *belief* state, *i.e.*, the state that the agent believes it is in. Therefore, we can map S_{MKV} to the set of BDI belief states, for which we write Bel_S. The exclusion of desires and intentions is not an obstacle in this correspondence because they are data structures that are internal to the agent, and therefore are unrelated to the state of the environment.

As we can see, we have established a mapping of the components that are clearly related in each model. The rest of this chapter is dedicated to establishing a mapping between the most important components of each model: *intentions* (and i-plans, as discussed below) on the BDI side, and *policies* on the MDP side. They are considered the most important because they dictate how the respective agents will behave; therefore, a mapping between these components will also involve rewards on the MDP side, and desires on the BDI side.

4.2 Intentions, i-plans, and Policies

In the basic BDI model (as discussed in Chapter 2), intentions were presented as "the agent's current focus, *i.e.*, those states to which it is committed to arrive". Intentions are generated by the *filter* functions and then an i-plan is constructed to satisfy a selected intention. According to the correspondence in Section 4.1, i-plans are sequences of actions from an agent's action set. Since actions map between states, we can think of the state-space $\langle S, A \rangle$ as a directed hypergraph with every node labeled by a state, and the hyperedges between nodes being labeled by actions. We can think of a sequence of states:

$$s_0, s_1, \ldots, s_n$$

as defining a path through this hypergraph. Given the fact that transitions between states are controlled by actions, it is most useful to deal with what we will call *trajectories*, sequences of states annotated where actions are associated with each state.

Definition 4.1. Let S be a state space, A be an action space, $s_0, \ldots, s_n \in S$, and $a_0, \ldots, a_{n-1} \in A$. A *trajectory* is an alternating sequence τ of the form

$$s_0, a_0, s_1, a_1, \ldots, s_{n-1}, a_{n-1}, s_n$$

We say that τ is *feasible* if and only if for all $0 \le i < n$, $s_{i+1} \in a_i(s_i)$. We use the term "f-trajectory" to denote a feasible trajectory.

As in (Thrun et al, 2001) we can specify, without loss of generality, that certain actions are the actions of specific agents or changes to the environment — for example in a single agent world, every odd-numbered action is a (possibly null) change in the environment — giving us a general model that fits as many agents as we choose to consider. We can also talk about sequences of actions:

$$a_0, a_1, \ldots, a_n$$

and such a sequence is a classical AI *plan*. We will denote such a plan as P. Now, a plan is typically conceived as being applied starting in a specific state, and executing a plan in a specific state s_0 will generate an f-trajectory. However, with non-deterministic actions, we will not know what this trajectory will be before we execute the actions — it is typically one of many trajectories that might be followed. However, what we can define before executing the actions is the set of all possible trajectories that might be traversed by a plan.

Definition 4.2. Let P be a sequence of actions $a_0, a_1, \ldots, a_n$. The *set of trajectories* of length $n \in \mathbb{N}$ starting in state s_0 associated with P, denoted $\mathscr{T}(P, s_0, n)$ is the set of all

$$s_0, a_0, S_1, a_1, \ldots S_{n-1}, a_{n-1}, S_n \tag{4.1}$$

where $S_i = \{s_j | s \in S_{i-1}, s_j \in a_{i-1}(s)\}$

In other words, each S_i in the definition above is the set of states that might be arrived in by applying the relevant action to each of the previous states. Thus, for a given $\langle S, A \rangle$, and a given initial state s_o, a plan P defines a set of trajectories all of which have s_0 as their start point.

An *i-plan* is a plan to achieve a specific intention, so in addition to an associated start state s_0, it has an intention that it is trying to achieve, and for us that is synonymous with saying that there is some final state, s_f that the *i*-plan is trying to reach.

Definition 4.3. Let S be a state space, A be an action space, and P be a plan over $\langle S, A \rangle$. An *i-plan* is a triple $\langle s_o, P, s_f \rangle$ where $s_0, s_f \in S$ are the start and end states, respectively. If plan P comprises n actions, we say that the i-plan is of length n.

Note that in Definition 4.3 above we assume that the agent plans to reach a specific state instead of a set of states that satisfy some condition. We adopted this definition for reasons of simplicity in the treatment that follows, and because it is the classical definition of linear plan. Intention reconsideration can, however, take into account the fact that a final state (or other states along the way) that is part of an i-plan is still equivalent, or good enough, for the purposes that gave rise to its creation. We refer the reader to our further discussion of this topic in Section 4.4.2 (Page 40).

When clear from the context, we will sometimes refer to the linear plan and the i-plan itself interchangeably. The initial state and the plan define, as above, a set of trajectories that result in a (possible) set of final states S_n. Looking at the sets of states gives us a way to assess i-plans.

Definition 4.4. Let $\psi = \langle s_o, P, s_f \rangle$ be an i-plan, J_P be its associated set of trajectories, and S_n be the set of all possible states in which trajectories in J_P end. We say that ψ is *sound* iff $s_f \in S_n$, that it is *singular* iff $|S_n| = 1$, and that it is *complete* iff it is both sound and singular.

Intuitively, a sound i-plan is capable of achieving the intention, a singular one will always end up in the same state, and a complete one is guaranteed to achieve the intention. We will also need to refer to sets of i-plans, sometimes imposing special properties on them such as the following.

Definition 4.5. Let Ψ be a set of i-plans over state space S and action space A. We say that Ψ is an *independent* set of i-plans if and only if there do not exist $\psi_i = \langle s_i, P_i, t_i \rangle$ and $\psi_j = \langle s_j, P_j, t_j \rangle$ in Ψ such that $\psi_i \neq \psi_j$ and $s_i = s_j$.

Intuitively, a set of i-plans is independent if all plans have different starting state.

Definition 4.6. Let Ψ be a set of i-plans over state space S and action space A. We say that Ψ *fully covers* S if and only if for each $s \in S$ there exists $\psi = \langle s, P, t \rangle$ in Ψ.

In the following, we will use the following notation: an i-plan will be denoted with a lowercase Greek letter such as ψ and we denote the i-th action in ψ with ψ_i. Similarly, we note the i-th state in the trajectory plotted when ψ was created (*i.e.*, the states that the agent plans to visit while executing ψ) as s_i^ψ. Therefore, for an i-plan ψ of length p, the agent starts at state s_0^ψ and plans on subsequently visiting states $s_1^\psi, s_2^\psi, \ldots s_p^\psi$; we will call this f-trajectory the *ideal* trajectory associated with ψ. It should be noted that this sequence of states is what the agent *plans* to visit; it may very well be that case that, because of some unwanted outcome of an action or changes in the environment, the agent ends up visiting other states before finishing the execution of the actions in ψ. For example, if the agent is currently in state s_7, and plans to carry out a series of four actions in order to reach state s_{82}, its i-plan might define the following ideal f-trajectory:

$$s_7 \xrightarrow{a_3} s_5 \xrightarrow{a_8} s_{33} \xrightarrow{a_1} s_{79} \xrightarrow{a_2} s_{82}$$

If we consider environments in which actions are not deterministic, it is possible that the full execution of an *i*-plan will not have the desired effect. In these cases, the probability of success for a given *i*-plan will depend on the probability of success of the individual actions that make it up. It is here where intention reconsideration becomes an important part of the agent's behavior. When the agent realizes that its intentions are no longer adequate, *i.e.*, that it is in a state that is somehow deviated from the plan, it must deliberate so it does not *waste effort*.

The expected *value* (or utility) of executing a plan can be obtained by means of a simple calculation involving the expected utility of executing the actions in the plan, which considers all of the possible states in which the agent might end up while executing the actions, and their utilities. We shall see an example of how this can be done in Section 4.4.

In this framework, a *policy* is still a simple mapping from state to action:

$$\pi : S \mapsto A$$

It is natural to think about the relationship between policies and trajectories. Clearly if we are given a policy, we can easily *generate* a trajectory.

Definition 4.7. Let π be a policy over state space S and action space A, $s_0 \in S$, and $n \in \mathbb{N}$. A trajectory of length n *generated* by policy π starting from state s_0 is any trajectory:

$$s_0, a_0, s_1, a_1, \ldots, s_{n-1}, a_{n-1}, s_n$$

where for all $0 \le i < n$, $\pi(s_i) = a_i$ and $s_{i+1} \in a_i(s_i)$

Intuitively, the trajectory that is generated by a policy is just a trajectory where every action is the one picked by the policy. This, of course, is the precise trajectory generated by one specific run of the policy. Other executions of the policy starting in the same state will generate other runs (since actions are non-deterministic), and the complete set of runs that can possibly be generated is the trajectory set defined by the policy.

Definition 4.8. Let π be a policy over state space S and action space A, and $n \in \mathbb{N}$. The *set of trajectories* of length n starting from state $s_0 \in S$ associated with π, denoted $\mathscr{T}(\pi, s_0, n)$ is the set of all trajectories

$$s_0, a_0, S_1, a_1, \ldots S_{n-1}, a_{n-1}, S_n$$

where $0 \le i < n$, $\pi(s_i) = a_i$ and $S_i = \{s_j \mid s \in S_{i-1}, s_j \in a_{i-1}(s)\}$.

That is, set $\mathscr{T}(\pi, s_0, n)$ is defined exactly as for plans (cf. Definition 4.2), but with each action picked by π. There is thus some kind of relationship between a plan P and a policy π since each defines a trajectory set. The main difference between them is that with a plan, at least as defined here, the actions are decided ahead of time, whereas when we execute a policy, the choice of action at a particular step is contingent on the state. Of course, the kind of trajectory set we have considered as being generated by a policy is a very particular kind — it has a specific start state and it is only a fixed number of states long. We will refer to a trajectory set that is rooted in a single state like this as a *single state* trajectory set, and one that is limited so that it only has a specific number of actions we will call a *limited* trajectory set. A trajectory set that is limited to n actions will be called an n-*limited* trajectory set. In general we do not consider policies as applying in this kind of way. Rather, policies specify an action in any state and do not have a sense of "end". Rather they continue execution and trajectories have a natural end in absorbing states[1].

When we consider a given trajectory set J and a given policy π, we can compare J with the trajectory set generated by following the policy. Since a policy specifies an action for every state, the *complete* trajectory set generated by a policy is the set of all trajectories that one gets by going through all the states one by one, and for each one generating the single-state trajectory set that results from following the policy starting at that state.

Definition 4.9. Let J be a set of trajectories of length $n \in \mathbb{N}$ and π be a policy over state space S and action space A. We say that J is *generatively equivalent* to π if and only if (1) for every $\tau \in J$, then $\tau \in \mathscr{T}(\pi, s, n)$ for some $s \in S$; and (2) for every $s \in S$, if $\tau \in \mathscr{T}(\pi, s, n)$ then $\tau \in J$.

Intuitively, this means says that a set of trajectories is generatively equivalent (or g-equivalent) to a policy if the trajectory set is exactly the complete set of trajectories generated by the policy. This allows us to relate a plan and a policy, as follows.

Definition 4.10. Let $\psi = \langle s_o, P, s_f \rangle$ be an i-plan of length $n \in \mathbb{N}$ and π be a policy over state space S and actions space A. We say that ψ and π *agree* if and only if ψ is g-equivalent to π.

In other words the i-plan and the policy agree if for every state that the plan might reach from its initial state onwards, the policy picks the next action in the plan. This is obviously a rather strong requirement, and weaker relationships are also useful, such as the following.

Definition 4.11. Let $\psi = \langle s_o, P, s_f \rangle$ be an i-plan of length $n \in \mathbb{N}$ and π be a policy over state space S and actions space A. We say that ψ and π are *compatible* if and only if $\mathscr{T}(P, s_0, n) \cap \mathscr{T}(\pi, s_0, n) \neq \emptyset$.

In other words, we say that an i-plan and a policy are compatible if at least one possible trajectory generated by the i-plan is part of the trajectory set of the policy. Finally, it will be of interest to our efforts to investigate the relationship between the ideal trajectory associated with an i-plan and a policy.

Definition 4.12. Let $\psi = \langle s_o, P, s_f \rangle$ be an i-plan of length $n \in \mathbb{N}$, with ideal associated trajectory $\tau^* = s_0, a_0, s_1, a_1, ...s_{n-1}, a_{n-1}, s_n$, and π be a policy over state space S and actions space A. We say that ψ *obeys* π if and only if for every $0 \leq i < n$, $a_i = \pi(s_i)$; conversely, we say that π *conforms* to ψ if and only if, for every $0 < i < n$, $\pi(s_i) = a_i$ for every s_i in the ideal trajectory associated with P.

---

[1] If such things exist. It is possible to imagine state spaces in which, like the journey of the Flying Dutchman, a trajectory never ends.

Since an *i*-plan is indexed by the intention that it will achieve when executed, we can extend the notions of obedience and conformance to intentions. A policy π conforms to an intention *i* if for all *i*-plans ψ built in order to achieve *i*, π conforms to ψ, and an intention *i* obeys a policy π if all such *i*-plans obey π.

According to Definition 4.12, an *i*-plan obeys a policy if its ideal trajectory picks the same actions as the policy in every state in the ideal trajectory (though off the ideal trajectory the *i*-plan may pick different actions than the policy), and a policy conforms to an *i*-plan if it picks the same action as the *i*-plan does along its ideal trajectory (but may pick different actions for states other than those along the ideal-trajectory). Therefore, a policy and an *i*-plan agree if the *i*-plan obeys the policy and the policy conforms to the *i*-plan.

These concepts will be useful in the rest of this chapter when we explore how the notions of *i*-plan and policy are related from the point of view of how one can be obtained from the other.

4.3 Potential Equivalence of Models

Now that we have seen that state spaces, actions, and transitions among states in MDPs can be directly mapped into their counterparts in BDI, we are ready to argue that, in theory, these models can be considered equivalent with respect to *how well they are capable of performing* in their environments; we have devoted Sections 4.4 and 4.5 below to providing the argument supporting this conclusion.

An Intuitive Argument

We have already pointed out that the computational edge that BDI sometimes has over MDPs is due to the flexibility of the BDI model. Its various components can be implemented as the designer sees fit, trading off optimality for computational tractability if necessary. This means that more complex problems can be treated by tractable heuristics, while simpler problems can be solved exactly. Therefore, in principle, a BDI agent's deliberation and means-ends reasoning components could be implemented using a decision theoretic model such as an MDP. In this case, the BDI model would "encapsulate" the MDP model, and would therefore behave exactly like an agent implemented by an MDP. We can then conclude that the BDI architecture is *at least as general* as the MDP model as it stands. As we will see below, we can argue the reverse as well, concluding that both models are actually equally expressive.

However, without going as far as implementing the BDI reasoning components with MDPs, it is still possible to see that deliberation and means-ends reasoning components built in such a way as to take into account the stochastic, unobservable, and dynamic nature of the environment are capable of producing intentions that lead the agent to a performance measure that is the same as that of an MDP agent. That is, it is viable to conceive of a BDI agent with deliberation and means-ends reasoning components implemented with MEU optimality in mind. However, as we have mentioned before, intention reconsideration is a key issue in obtaining such optimality; the formation of intentions with MEU is only half of the process. There are many ways in which intention reconsideration can be performed. For instance, (Schut, 2002) provides a decision-theoretic treatment of this process; the more recent work of (Fagundes et al, 2009) applies Bayesian Networks towards solving the problem, while (Tan et al, 2010) applies neural networks as part of the agent architecture that addresses this issue.

4.4 From Policies to i-plans

Assume we have a policy π that is the solution to a fully specified Markov Decision Process. It is important to note at this point that we are assuming that π is optimal; the initial theoretical mapping depends on this assumption. We will see, later on, that this assumption can be dropped, and a set of intentions can also be extracted from an arbitrary policy. Once we have a policy, we will use the well known fact that it is possible to extract utility values for the MDP's states such that they induce π. These values are at the center of the mappings that we will define in the following sections.

For the purposes of this section, we shall consider a policy π to be the result obtained by the convergence of an algorithm such as Q-Learning (which works with mappings of state-action pairs into real numbers). Now, the BDI agent can also map states and actions into values. These values can be computed by assigning a value (utility) to each intention. Let $\psi = \langle s_0, P, s_f \rangle$ be an i-plan of length p, and ψ_i the i-th action involved in ψ. One way of assigning a value to ψ is[2]:

$$V(\psi) = \sum_{i=1}^{p} \frac{R\left(s_{i-1}^{\psi}, \psi_i\right)}{i} \tag{4.2}$$

where $V(\psi)$ is the value of i-plan ψ, s_{i+1}^{ψ} is the state in which the agent *expects* to arrive after executing action ψ_i (*i.e.*, the $i+1$-th state in the ideal trajectory), and $R(s_{i-1}^{\psi}, \psi_i)$ is the reward received for taking action ψ_i in state s_{i-1}^{ψ}. Therefore, the value assigned to an i-plan is the sum of rewards that will be achieved if all of the actions have the desired effect. The division of the reward by i in the above formula is a form of time-discounting (Boutilier et al, 1999) — it represents the fact that rewards gained early are more valuable than the ones gained in the future. It is important to note that this is only one way of assigning a value to an i-plan. In general, we only require that, all other things being equal, for an i-plan ψ, the value that is added by action ψ_i is greater than the value added by action ψ_j, if $i < j$, and that these values depend on the rewards of the states that the agent plans to visit.

---

[2] Other ways of doing this come to mind, such as different discounting strategies; for the sake of simplicity, we will adopt Formula 4.2 for the purpose of this section.

For example, in the TILEWORLD environment, the reward function can be defined simply by:

$$R\left(s_{i-1}^{\psi}, \psi_i\right) = \begin{cases} 1 & \text{if } \psi_i \text{ leads to a hole,} \\ 0 & \text{otherwise.} \end{cases}$$

and $R(s, a) = 0$ for every other state/action pair.

Definition 4.12 simply states that an *i*-plan obeys a policy if, and only if, the actions prescribed by the *i*-plan are the same as those prescribed by the policy through the *i*-plan's intermediate states. The notion of conformance is the dual of the notion of obedience. Remember that we are assuming that BDI agents' *i*-plans are built as *linear* plans, *i.e.*, that no considerations are made for unexpected outcomes of actions. Now, based on the concepts that were introduced above, we are prepared to make the following claim:

Claim. Given a BDI agent and an MDP agent with an optimal policy π, if the BDI agent is in state s, then the *i*-plan ψ with the highest utility value will be such that ψ obeys π, starting at s.

In general, this will only hold if states with the same reward are considered in the same order by both algorithms. Otherwise, even though the utilities are equivalent, the actions might not be exactly the same because the order in which states with the same reward are considered can affect the selection of actions. The proof of this claim can be made with respect to progressively more complex scenarios (considering deterministic, non deterministic, fully accessible, partially accessible domains, etc). Our initial version of the mapping from policies to intentions is therefore established for the deterministic, fully accessible case:

Proposition 4.1. *Let* $A_{\text{MDP}} = (S, A, R, T)$ *be an* MDP *agent, where S is the state space, A is the set of possible actions, R is the reward function, and T is the state transition function. Let* π *be a policy that is optimal under the* MEU *criterion for* A_{MDP}. *Let* $A_{\text{BDI}} = (S', A, Bel, Des, Int)$ *be a BDI agent, where S' is the agent's set of states, Bel, Des, and Int hold the agent's current beliefs, desires, and intentions, respectively, and the rest of the components are equal to those of* A_{MDP}, *as discussed in Section 4.1. Let D represent* A_{BDI}'s *deliberation component, and M represent its means-ends reasoning component, where M is also optimal in the sense that it always selects the i-plan with the highest utility. If we consider that, for all* $s \in S$ *and* $a \in A, |T(s, a)| = 1$ *(that is, the environment is deterministic) then for all* $i \in Int$ *it holds that i obeys* π.

Proof. The result follows directly from the fact that we are assuming that M is optimal and that actions are completely deterministic in the environment. Because π is MEU optimal, it will always select actions that take the agent to the best goal in the best possible way. Because of the way in which we have defined utilities over intentions, this goal will yield the maximum utility, and will therefore be selected by M during intention formation, using the best actions possible. Therefore, if we assume that states with equal rewards are considered in the same order by π and M, it is clear that the *i*-plans generated by M will contain linear plans that contain the best possible actions, which means that the *i*-plan obeys π. $\qquad \square$

If actions are not deterministic, the utility of intentions is not so clearly defined. Instead of a simple summation of rewards along the path of the plan, the *failure* of actions must be considered. Therefore, we must now assume that the means-ends reasoning component is also MEU optimal (it was also trivially MEU optimal in the deterministic case).

Proposition 4.2. *Let* $A_{\text{MDP}} = (S, A, R, T)$ *be an* MDP *agent,* π *be a policy, and* $A_{\text{BDI}} = (S', A, Bel, Des, Int)$ *be a* BDI *agent, as in Proposition 4.1. Assume that in general* $|T(s,a)| \geq 1$, *thus the environment is non deterministic, and that M* (A_{BDI}*'s means-ends reasoning component) is MEU-optimal. Then, for all* $i \in Int$ *it holds that* i *obeys* π.

Proof. This result is similar to the previous one, but considering that actions may fail. Because we are now assuming that M builds i-plans that are MEU-optimal, it follows directly that every i-plan will contain actions selected in the same way in which those of π are, and therefore such i-plans obey π. □

In the case in which the environment is not fully observable, the agent must rely on its estimates of the current state of the environment, and we now have POMDPs instead of MDPs. Because the correspondence we saw between the MDP's state space and the BDI agent's belief states clearly extends to POMDPs, it can be stated that i-plans built by BDI agents in this type of environment also obey the POMDP's policy.

Proposition 4.3. *Let* $A_{\text{POMDP}} = (S, A, R, T, Z, O)$ *be a* POMDP *agent,* π *be an optimal policy,* $A_{\text{BDI}} = (S', A, Bel, Des, Int)$ *be a* BDI *agent, as in Proposition 4.1, with the addition of a set Z of observations, and a function O corresponding to a probability distribution over Z. Assume that in general* $|T(s,a)| \geq 1$, *that the environment is partially observable, and that M* (A_{BDI}*'s means-ends reasoning component) is MEU-optimal. Then, for all* $i \in Int$ *it holds that* i *obeys* π.

Proof. This result generalizes the previous ones because we are now considering a partially observable environment. However, as we discussed in Chapter 2, the state space for A_{BDI} corresponds to a set of *belief states*, as in the case of A_{POMDP}. Therefore, because M builds i-plans that are MEU-optimal, it follows that partial observability is considered equally under both models, and therefore $\forall i \in Int$, it holds that i obeys π. □

We have therefore established an initial mapping from policies to intentions and i-plans, similar to the one informally discussed in Section 4.3. Even though we must make some assumptions in order to be able to prove the equivalence, the results in this section are important because they establish that a relationship in fact *exists* between the models. We will now explore a *computational* view of the mapping, which poses no such restrictions in order to be applicable (and which, as a result, need not generate optimal i-plans or policies).

Another way of establishing a relationship between intentions and policies is to *derive* an i-plan from a policy. This can be done by tracing a path from the current state to a goal (which is a state that receives a specific reward in the MDP, and is

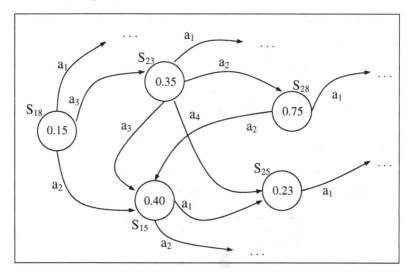

Fig. 4.1 Part of the state space of an MDP

therefore considered a goal); this state can be identified by means of a simple search through the state space, following policy π until a local maximum is reached[3]. As stated in Definition 4.7 above, this yields a trajectory that is generated by π, from which a linear plan can directly be extracted. Now, by following policy π in this manner, we are able to obtain as many *i*-plans as desired: after reaching a goal state, simply continue following the policy from the state that results after achieving the previous goal. For example, in Figure 4.1 we illustrate this by analyzing a fragment of a state space of an MDP. Assume the agent is currently in state S_{18}, $\pi(S_{18}) = a_3$, and $\pi(S_{23}) = a_2$, and that state S_{28} is a goal for the agent. The *i*-plan that can be extracted in this situation is the linear plan $\langle a_3, a_2 \rangle$. In this case, the *i*-plan that arises is obtained as the result of only one iteration of the process. The same is true in the case of the simplified TILEWORLD considered in Chapter 3, where agents only build plans for reaching one hole, and not multiple hole tours. Figure 4.2 outlines the process just described in an algorithm `policyToIPlan` in a JAVA-like pseudocode.

It should be clear that we are now exploring the relationship that exists between *arbitrary policies* in MDPs and *i*-plans in BDI. Such policies are not necessarily optimal, they are just mappings of states into actions used by agents to govern their behavior. Because the BDI model does not consider stochastic actions (it assumes actions always have the desired effect), it is possible for an *i*-plan not to succeed, causing the agent to drift from the sequence of states that it was planning to visit. Intention reconsideration can therefore be required when the agent realizes that the current state is not one of the states that belong to its current intention (the path from

---

[3] In order to select a unique goal using this process, we assume that the agent's actions are always successful; otherwise, a tree would result instead of a simple path.

```
Intention policyToIplan(Policy π, MDP m) {
    Iplan i;
    s = getCurrentState(m);
    g = getGoalState(s,π,m);
    p = obtainPath(s,g,m);
    while not empty(p) do {
        i.addAction(p);
        p.deleteAction();
    }
    return i;
}
```

Fig. 4.2 Pseudocode for mapping policies into intentions

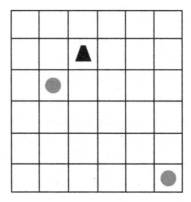

Fig. 4.3 A hole appears to the far Southeast.

the state it was in when it made the plan to a goal state). An optimal reconsideration strategy *with respect to the policy* being considered can then be defined so that the agent reconsiders when the policy dictates a different action than the one being taken. As we can see, this intention reconsideration policy dictates that the agent must deliberate when a change has occurred in the current state that has rendered the intention sub-optimal. Note that changes due to the dynamic characteristics of the environment do not necessarily induce intention reconsideration. Consider the example in Figure 4.3, in which the agent (represented by the black shape) has the goal of reaching the hole that is one cell away, to the Southwest, and a hole has just appeared in the Southeast corner. In this example, even though a change has occurred in the environment (and therefore the current state has changed), the agent's *i*-plan is still optimal, and intention reconsideration in this case would be a case of wasted effort. On the other hand, consider the example in Figure 4.4, in which the agent wishes to reach the hole that is three cells North from its current position. After performing the first action in its plan, it accidently moves West, and its *i*-plan is now clearly suboptimal. The best thing to do would then be to reconsider, which would lead to a new *i*-plan.

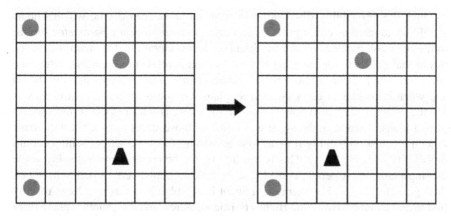

Fig. 4.4 The agent moves West while trying to move North.

The following proposition establishes the relationship between the input and the output of Algorithm `policyToIplan`.

Proposition 4.4. *Let π be a policy over state space S and action space A, and m be an MDP over the same domain. The output of* `policyToIplan`(π, m) *is an i-plan that obeys π.*

Proof. Follows directly from the definition of obedience and the way in which the algorithm constructs the linear plan by following the policy. □

4.4.1 Obtaining 'more universal' i-plans

As we have seen, state transitions that disagree with the agent's *i*-plans may occur both because of the dynamic character of the environment and because of non-determinism in the execution of actions. In order to deal with the latter problem, we can build *i*-plans that are *more universal* (in the sense that they allow for contingencies). Such *i*-plans can be built by obtaining a probability distribution over the state space that represents the probability of arriving at a given state by following a given policy, and re-planning from those states. This distribution can be built by dividing the state space into two classes: states that are reachable by faulty action (that is, there exists a failure that leads to this state), and the rest. If a state is not reachable, then its probability will be zero. Otherwise, the probability is obtained as the probability of the occurrence of the failure that leads to it. Only one failure should be considered; after a failure, the agent realizes that it is not in the state it should be in, and adopts another *i*-plan (one of the contingencies). In relation to the concepts presented in Section 4.2, if we take the union of all the sets of trajectories induced by *i*-plans in a collection obtained in this way, the set of trajectories will be *compatible* with those of the policy used.

Once this probability distribution is built, the agent can decide which *i*-plans should be adopted as contingencies, according to a *contingency parameter* similar to the boldness parameter used for intention reconsideration. The main difference lies in that boldness for intention reconsideration is related to the agent's *dynamic* behavior, which dictates under which situations the agent engages in deliberation and when it decides to carry on with its plans. On the other hand, contingency is a static concept related to how optimistic the agent is with respect to the success of its *i*-plans. Therefore, the agent will consider those states to which it will arrive at with greatest probability if its actions go wrong, for those actions with a certain probability of being faulty. This is inspired by the behavior humans display while making plans; most people consider, after making plans, certain points in which their plans might fail. For example, if agent Paul's plan is to travel to New York by first taking a plane from Bahía Blanca to Buenos Aires, and then another plane from Buenos Aires to New York, it might consider the first step to be error prone due to frequent delays due to fog and storms. Therefore, it could plan for the contingency of not being able to get to Buenos Aires by plane by planning to take a bus. This type of reasoning is carried out constantly by human beings, because it saves time in the event of actions not turning out as they were expected.

The literature on *contingent planning* is relevant to this problem; see (Goldman et al, 2009; Albore et al, 2009; Geffner, 2010). Finding ways to combine approaches to contingent planning in both MDPs and BDI is an interesting problem that might shed more light on the discussion above.

4.4.2 State Spaces and Heuristics

The analysis above established a relationship between BDI and MDP models based on the existence in the BDI agent's plan library of *i*-plans that lay out a precise sequence of actions that the agent has to carry out. It turns out that the *i*-plans that a BDI agent are typically equipped with aren't quite so detailed. Consider the typical algorithms used for solving MDPs, or learning algorithms such as Q-learning. What these algorithms basically do is "sweep" the state space, assigning utility values either to states themselves or to state-action pairs. Even though there exists great variety in the workings of these algorithms, there is one invariant among them: *they consider each state separately* in their computations. By this we mean that, for decision-theoretic algorithms, two separate states are considered to be *completely unrelated*, no matter how similar they are with respect to the situation they are describing.

On the other hand, what happens in a typical BDI implementation is that the deliberation process decides *what* is to be achieved — what intention to adopt. Once a decision is made, the means-ends reasoning process then decides *how* this will be achieved — what *i*-plan will be used — picking from a set of relatively abstract *i*-plans and instantiating it to fit the specific situation. The result is to effectively groups states into "envelopes" which contain sets of states that are equivalent as far

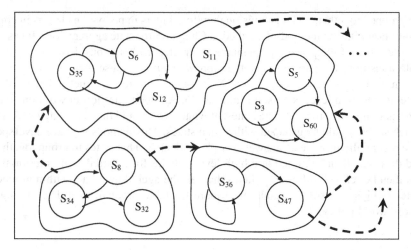

Fig. 4.5 Grouping of states into "envelopes".

as the current intention of the agent is concerned but which might differ in detail. For example, considering Figure 4.5, imagine that each state represents an agent location. The agent is currently at s_{34} and needs to get to s_{60}, and its environment is split into a series of rooms that group states together — s_{34} with s_8 and s_{32}, all in the same room but at different levels of illumination, say — and so on. Now the important thing as far as the agent is concerned, while navigating around, is which room it is in, so it can construct an *i*-plan at the "room level", figuring that it needs to get to the $\langle s_{36}, s_{47} \rangle$ room first, then to the $\langle s_3, s_5, s_{60} \rangle$ room; the dashed lines in this case indicate transitions among states that belong to different envelopes. The BDI agent's deliberation component effectively induces a partition on the state space into *equivalence classes*. While the agent is in any state within an equivalence class, all is well because the *i*-plans it has selected are still valid[4]. Now, if the agent *involuntarily* passes from one state to a state that is not in the same class, its *i*-plans will no longer be valid, as in the example in Figure 4.4.

The idea of grouping states in MDPs and POMDPs is not new, as we will discuss in Chapter 5. However, it does tie in very neatly with the BDI model, and we can easily see that it will be possible to establish similar results to those we have obtained above, but where the correspondence is not between whole-environment policies and *i*-plans at the level of individual states, but between *i*-plans and policies at the state-aggregation level.

From this discussion we can conclude that, while decision theoretic planning is concerned with every transition from state to state, heuristic planning groups states into equivalence classes and considers transitions from class to class. Now, this grouping is done *automatically* by the agent (in the case of human beings, one would say *subconsciously*); there is no explicit process by means of which the states

---

[4] This is directly related to the point made after Definition 4.3 (Page 30) regarding why *i*-plans are assumed to have a single finalizing state instead of a class of states.

are grouped together, and this division therefore incurs in no overhead costs in computation (unlike the methods described in Chapter 5 for state aggregation). It is simply the result of the process of planning abstractly, without considering every possible transition; the partitions are therefore *dynamic*, because they are completely determined by the current intention. Now, being able to construct policies at the state-aggregation level is a useful thing to do. An open question in work on state-aggregation is how to aggregate states, at what level should they be aggregated, and which states should be grouped with which states. The methods we have developed here potentially provide an answer — *i*-plans identify what states to group together, and these can then be turned into high-level policies for a partial MDP solution that can then be refined, filling in policies that tell the agent how to act within grouped states (which is a smaller, and hence more tractable problem than determining a whole-world policy).

4.5 From *i*-plans to Policies

In this section, we will explore the other side of the mapping introduced in Section 4.4. A method is studied for assigning rewards to states in such a way that solving the resulting MDP provides a policy that mimics the behavior of an agent with the given *i*-plans. In Section 4.5.1 we introduce the mapping in theory, while in Section 4.5.2 we look at a closely related mapping from a computational point of view, providing simple examples of how it works in order to present an appropriate illustration. Lastly, in Section 4.5.3, we generalize the results in the previous sections in order to provide a full mapping from BDI to MDPs, *i.e.*, a mapping from the deliberation and means-ends reasoning components to policies.

4.5.1 Theoretical Mapping

We will start off by showing how rewards can be assigned in the state space in order to map *one* *i*-plan into a policy. Later on, we will see how the process is generalized to an arbitrary set of *i*-plans.

Assume the agent is currently in state s_a, and has adopted some *i*-plan ψ of length p. Then, we can assign a value to each state-action pair according to the following formula:

$$val\left(s_{i-1}^{\psi}, \psi_i\right) \stackrel{def}{=} i \cdot U(\psi) \tag{4.3}$$

$\forall i, 1 \leq i \leq p$, s_i^{ψ} is the *i*-th state involved in ψ, and ψ_i is the *i*-th action in ψ. In any other case, we have

$$val\left(s_j, a_k\right) \stackrel{def}{=} 0 \tag{4.4}$$

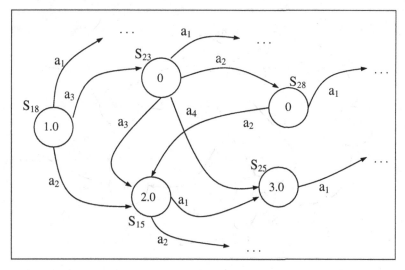

Fig. 4.6 Part of a state space, with values assigned to the states leading to a goal.

$\forall s_j \neq s_i^\psi$, for any s_i^ψ such that $1 \leq i \leq p$, $\forall a_k$. These values induce a policy that can be directly obtained by selecting the action with the highest value given the current state. This process marks a path through the state-space for the agent assuming that nothing will go wrong. Such a policy only considers what to do in states that are involved in ψ, and therefore allows for no error in the execution of actions. If, instead of assigning values to state-action pairs we want to assign values to states only, we can use a variation of the *val* function as defined above:

$$val'\left(s_{i-1}^\psi\right) \overset{def}{=} i \cdot U(\psi)$$

$\forall i, 1 \leq i \leq p$, s_i^ψ is the *i*-th state involved in ψ, and

$$val'(s_j) \overset{def}{=} 0$$

$\forall s_j \neq s_i^\psi$, for any s_i^ψ such that $1 \leq i \leq p$.

This mapping of states into values is then used as the reward function, which will clearly mark the path that the agent must follow in order to reach the goal. This reward function will lead an MDP solution technique that obtains an optimal policy to execute *i*-plan ϕ. It can be argued that assigning rewards to states with the objective of "leading the agent towards the solution" is not a good practice, because the problem is not being formulated purely, but incorporating part of the solution into the specification (Sutton and Barto, 1998; Errecalde, 2003). However, because our objective is to draw a mapping between models, this drawback is not applicable in our case. In Figure 4.6, we show this assignment of values to states for the fragment of state space from Figure 4.1. The agent is initially in state S_{18}, and has formed the intention of reaching state S_{25} by executing actions a_2 and a_1.

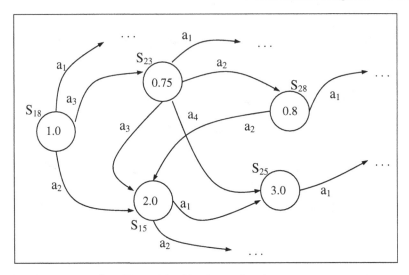

Fig. 4.7 The state space from Figure 4.6, with values assigned to every state.

Therefore, if we assume that each action has unit cost, state S_{18} is given the value 1.0, S_{15} is given 2.0, and the goal is given 3.0; the rest of the states are assigned the value 0.

Proposition 4.5. *Let* $\psi = \langle s_0, P, s_f \rangle$ *be an i-plan of length n. A policy derived from the utility values described by Equations 4.3 and 4.4 w.r.t.* ψ *conforms to* ψ.

Proof. The result follows directly from the fact that the values describe a sequence of monotonically increasing utility values associated with ψ's ideal trajectory. Therefore, the induced policy trivially conforms to ψ.   □

Up to now, the mapping we have presented maps an *i*-plan to its "equivalent" in terms of policies. That is, we have only obtained a correspondence from states to actions similar to the one described in Section 4.2. This does not consider what to do in cases in which the agent *drifts from the path* of its initial *i*-plan. Notice that, using the values described in Equations 4.3 and 4.4, we can easily obtain a policy that agrees with an *i*-plan by "branching out" the assignment of values to each possible trajectory from the starting state. However, if we want to obtain a policy that genuinely considers every possible contingency and corrects unexpected state transitions, this can be done by fully solving the MDP by means of any of the existing algorithms. These will "fill-in" the values of states without associated utilities by considering the expected cost of getting from those states to ones that already have utilities associated with them. The example in Figure 4.7 illustrates how the rest of the states now have associated utilities. As a direct consequence of Proposition 4.5, such a policy will also conform to the associated *i*-plan.

```
Policy iplanToPolicy(IplanSet I, BDI A) {
    MDP m;
    Policy π;
    ValueFunction val;
    int κ, j = 0;

    val.initialize(0);
    m.initialize(A);
    orderedIplan = I.obtainOrdering();
    for each i in orderedIplan do {
        j = 0;
        for each action a in i do {
            s = i.obtainInvolvedState(j++);
            val.setState(s,a) = κ*i.getUtil();
            κ++;
        }
    }
    π = valueIteration(m,val);
    return π;
}
```

Fig. 4.8 Pseudocode for mapping *i*-plans into policies

4.5.2 General Mapping

In order to use the same technique when an agent has more than one *i*-plan, only a minor change needs to be made. Instead of simply defining

$$val\left(s_{i-1}^{\psi}, \psi_i\right) \stackrel{def}{=} i \cdot U(\psi)$$

for actions in certain states, we must take into account that the *i*-plan being considered is not necessarily the first. Therefore, we must keep track of the number of actions involved in the *i*-plans that have already been processed, which will be represented by the letter κ. When the process starts, we set $\kappa = 1$, indicating that the action to be considered is the first. Therefore, function *val* is now defined:

$$val\left(s_{i-1}^{\psi}, \psi_i\right) \stackrel{def}{=} \kappa \cdot U(\psi) \tag{4.5}$$

$\forall i, 1 \leq i \leq p$, s_i is the *i*-th state involved in ψ, and ψ_i is the *i*-th action in ψ. After each action is considered, the value of κ is increased by 1. After all *i*-plans have been processed, we have

$$val(s_j, a_k) \stackrel{def}{=} 0 \tag{4.6}$$

$\forall s_j \neq s_i$, for any s_i involved in some intention, $\forall a_k$. Suppose, for example, that the agent has two *i*-plans ψ and φ, of lengths p and q, respectively. After processing ψ, κ will have the value $p+1$ and, after processing φ, its value will be $p+q+1$. This process is outlined in Figure 4.2, which presents algorihtm `iPlanToPolicy` in a JAVA-like pseudocode.

The following proposition formalizes the relationship between a set of *i*-plans and a policy as established by this algorithm:

Proposition 4.6. *The algorithm* `iplanToPolicy` *obtains a policy which conforms to each i-plan in the given set.*

Proof. The algorithm considers each *i*-plan in the set in turn, assigning a value to each state-action pair that is involved in the *i*-plan's ideal trajectory. The value that is assigned is the product of the current *i*-plan's utility and a monotonically increasing succession of integers. Therefore, each state-action pair will receive a monotonically increasing value with respect to the one before it. Up to this point we have an assignment of monotonically increasing values to the state-action pairs that the given set of *i*-plans dictates, which allows us to obtain a straightforward policy using these values. If we feed the value iteration algorithm with these value assignments, the rest of the state-action pairs (not involved in the set of intentions) will receive values according to this assignment. The value iteration algorithm ensures us that the resulting policy will be MEU with respect to the input values.   □

Even though this generalizes the process described for single *i*-plans, we must specify how the *i*-plans are ordered. As we have seen in Section 4.4, *i*-plans can be assigned utilities in relation with how their execution will reward the agent by reaching certain goals. Because *i*-plans in this model are sequences of actions that take the agent through the state space, they will naturally be ordered with respect to each other. The full set of *i*-plans therefore defines a "tour" of the state space. This need to specify a preference relationship among intentions is one of the drawbacks of decision-theoretic models, as we have mentioned before.

Using this last approach to assigning rewards, we can use Value Iteration as an *anytime* algorithm[5] to complete the values of the rest of the states. With each iteration, more and more states will receive non-zero values, making the plan more universal. The example in Figures 4.9 to 4.11 show how the algorithm evolves after three iterations. It should be noted that, because these examples are based on a partial view of a state space, the values shown are for illustrative purposes only.

4.5.3 Mapping Deliberation and Means-ends Reasoning into Policies

Up to now, we have only been considering the problem of how to map a single *i*-plan or a group of *i*-plans into a policy. Even though we have established a relationship between the most important components of both models, the mapping is not yet

---

[5] An anytime algorithm is one that produces a solution to a given problem immediately and progressively enhances the solution with time. If stopped *at any time*, it will return a solution (Dean and Boddy, 1988).

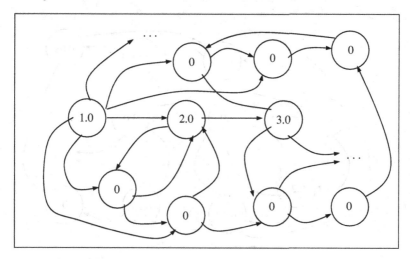

Fig. 4.9 State values after iteration 1.

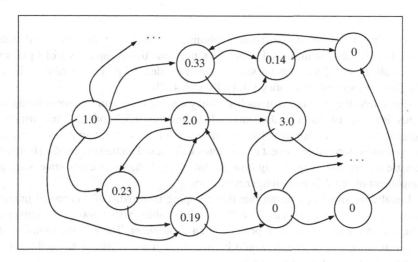

Fig. 4.10 State values after iteration 2.

complete because the policies obtained in Sections 4.5.1 and 4.5.2 correspond to "snapshots" of the BDI agent's state. Should the agent switch *i*-plans (for example, due to intention reconsideration performed in order to profit from a change in the environment), these policies would no longer be valid.

It is possible to map the *complete* set of possible *i*-plans into a single policy by considering what the BDI agent would do in every possible state. If deliberation is performed in *every* state, followed by means-ends reasoning, a policy can be built by assigning actions to states corresponding to what the BDI planner dictates. It is clear that this process need not be initiated in every state; if a state already has an action assigned to it (because a previously built plan runs through it), then there is

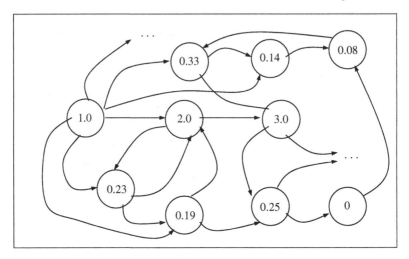

Fig. 4.11 State values after iteration 3.

no sense in performing the same computations again. Recalling the concepts defined in Section 4.2 (cf. Definitions 4.5 and 4.6), note that this complete set of i-plans is independent and fully covers the state space of the derived policy; moreover, the set of i-plans agrees with the policy (cf. Definition 4.10).

It is interesting to note that such a policy can be built without considering rewards. Rewards played a fundamental role in Sections 4.5.1 and 4.5.2 because they were the basis for the construction of *contingencies*; once the main plans were laid, the actions performed in the rest of the states were based on these rewards. However, because we are now considering how the BDI agent behaves in every state, such an assignment of rewards is no longer necessary.

Finally, we should point out that this mapping is initially of theoretical interest only, and its sole purpose is to show that a relationship exists between the universal behavior of a BDI agent and a policy for an MDP agent. The computational costs of constructing such a policy would be just as high as (or higher than) the actual process of solving the MDP directly.

Chapter 5
Related Work

In this work, we have presented a series of relationships that exist between certain components of the BDI model and those of MDPs. We have extended the work of (Schut et al, 2001) by exploring how *i-plans* on the BDI side and *policies* on the MDP side can be related to one another. To our knowledge, this is the first time that such a relationship has been proposed. There is, however, a rich body of work that is related to the research here presented.

5.1 The BDI model

The Belief-Desire-Intention model was established at least in part because it was felt that decision-theoretic models were too computationally intractable to use in practice (Bratman et al, 1991). This has led to a perception that the two models are somehow cast in opposition with one another, that one adopts the BDI model only if one believes that decision theoretic models are somehow wrong or impractical, and that to use BDI is to somehow settle for less than perfect performance (it is, after all, a heuristic approach). Our aim in this work is to show the existence of a middle path.

The BDI model has attracted much attention in the agents community since its introduction in (Bratman, 1987; Bratman et al, 1991). Many researchers have worked on topics related to this architecture, such as the following[1]:

- *Intention reconsideration* is one of the basic topics that needs to be addressed when designing BDI agents, as we discussed in the introduction. The experimental work of (Kinny and Georgeff, 1991) was pioneering in the area, and has in many ways influenced how researchers think about this problem. The problem was also attacked from a formal point of view in (Wooldridge and Parsons,

---

[1] This is of course an incomplete list, provided in the spirit of showing the diversity in the BDI literature.

1999), while (Schut and Wooldridge, 2000) extended previous experimental results. One of the first works to address the problem from a decision-theoretic point of view was that of (Schut et al, 2001). A good survey of the state of the art up until some years back can be found in (Schut et al, 2004). Some examples of recent novel developments in the area are the application of Bayesian networks in (Fagundes et al, 2009), and neural networks in (Tan et al, 2010).

- Reasoning and bounded rationality have also been topics of great interest since the model was proposed. The term *bounded rationality* in the autonomous agents domain refers to the problem agents face when trying to make decisions in the best way possible under constraints that usually prohibit the computation of optimal solutions. Rao and Georgeff were pioneers in this respect with there works in the early 1990s (Rao and Georgeff, 1991, 1995), as were Russell and Wefald around the same time (Russell and Wefald, 1992; Russell et al, 1993). Examples of more recent advances in this area are (Stroe et al, 2005), which attacks the problem of agent reasoning from the point of view of logic programs under the feasible status set semantics initially proposed in (Eiter et al, 1999), which was designed for the purpose of building agents on top of legacy code. The work of (Trigo and Coelho, 2008) addresses the problem of reasoning and bounded rationality in multi-agent environments, coming up with a hybrid between decision=theoretic and BDI approaches. For a recent and novel take on issues of rationality in agents, and how they can be compared to rationality in humans, see (Debenham and Sierra, 2010).

- Planning in BDI agents has seen much development in the last decade. Among some of the most relevant works, we have that of (Meneguzzi et al, 2004), which proposes the investigation of relationships between propositional planning and means-ends reasoning in BDI agents; (Sardiña et al, 2006) tackles the problem of the design of a formal semantics for an agent programming language for planning in BDI agents (incorporating the well known Hierarchical Task Networks (HTNs) planning formalism); also regarding agent programming languages, the work of (De Giacomo et al, 2010), addressing the problem of the computational complexity of executing agent programs. Finally, we would like to mention the works of (Barry et al, 2010) and (Teichteil-Konigsbuch et al, 2010), which adopt ideas in line with the ones presented in our work by addressing the problem of planning in MDPs by leveraging classical planners. We will discuss these works in more detail below.

- Finally, various implementations and tools that are based on the BDI model, the first of which was the PRS system (Georgeff and Ingrand, 1989) which evolved into the dMARS system (D'Inverno et al, July 2004). Another implementation of BDI ideas is the JACK Intelligent Agents suite (Busetta et al, 1999; Winikoff, 2005) that we used in this work. JACK provides tools useful in developing autonomous agents, including a superset of the JAVA language with support for BDI-style agents. There are many real-world systems that are using BDI in some form or another; for some recent examples, see (Burmeister et al, 2008; Sierhuis et al, 2009)

5.2 The MDP model

Markov Decision Processes were first presented in the Operations Research community (Bellman, 1957), and later adopted by many researchers for solving various sorts of decision problems. A comprehensive text on the subject is (Puterman, 1994), and (Lovejoy, 1991; Littman, 1996; Boutilier et al, 1999; Ferns et al, 2006; Hermanns et al, 2008; Barry et al, 2010; Kattenbelt et al, 2010) also cover in depth the topics of algorithms for solving both MDPs and POMDPs.

As we mentioned in Section 3.1, there have been many recent advances towards making MDPs more tractable; the following two broad techniques have been some of the most exploited towards this end:

State abstraction.

In Section 4.4.2 we discussed the idea of grouping states in such a way to abstract characteristics that are not important to the problem at hand. The idea of state aggregation is not a novel one; in fact, much work has been dedicated to the grouping of states in MDPs and POMDPs. The main idea behind state abstraction is to derive a smaller model with a corresponding loss of information (and thus optimality as well). An abstraction is basically defined by partitioning the set of "concrete" states (*i.e.*, the original states in the MDP into "abstract" states; the key problem is then to define a good partition in order to obtain a policy that approximates the original solution. The recently developed *counterexample-guided abstraction* refinement (CEGAR) technique (Hermanns et al, 2008) is a good example of how this problem can be addressed. Another state-of-the-art example of this technique is *quantitative abstraction refinement* (Kattenbelt et al, 2010). The concept of abstraction is also a well-known one in the Model Checking literature (Clarke et al, 1999). Other examples of this technique are our own basic approximations (see below).

The work of (Boutilier et al, 1999) provides a good survey of techniques based on state abstraction, aggregation, and decomposition based on classical representations from the AI literature. A more recent survey of this and other kinds of techniques to address scalability in MDPs and other probabilistic systems from the model checking point of view can be found in (Kwiatkowska et al, 2010).

Model reduction.

Apart from the abstraction techniques discussed above, there are other, more general techniques that focus on finding smaller models that can be used instead of the larger, unmanageable one. Some of these techniques exploit the symmetry present in the model, while others leverage state similarity to derive a smaller instance.

In (Dean et al, 1997), Dean, Givan, and Leach present a method for solving factored MDPs, based on the property of ε-homogeneity of state space partitions. Such partitions group together states that behave approximately the same under a certain set of policies, and define a family of related MDPs which have the state space equal to the *meta-states* in the aggregation, and transition probabilities similar to any of the states in the original MDP for any given meta-state. In this work, the authors also introduce the BDP (bounded parameter MDP) model, which is similar to classical MDPs, but have their transition probabilities and rewards defined in terms of upper and lower bounds. In (Goldsmith and Sloan, 2000), Goldsmith and Sloan show that the problem of transforming an MDP into a BDP (in particular, the test for ε-homogeneity), is coNP^{PP}-hard[2], which is a widely accepted indication that the method will not be directly applicable in practice. Other approaches to model reduction include *feature selection*, a technique that involves the participation of a domain expert that indicates which are the primary features that contribute to transition probabilities. This technique is analyzed by Tsitsiklis and Van Roy in (Tsitsiklis and van Roy, 1996). Even though part of the complexity is eliminated by introducing human participation, this does not mean that the problem is solved. In order for this technique to reduce complexity, few important features must exist so the others can be disregarded. Furthermore, the complexity results of Goldsmith and Sloan indicate that the problem is rooted at the test for ε-homogeneity, which means that the intractability of the technique does not depend on how the partition was obtained. Boutilier, Dearden, and Goldszmidt (Boutilier et al, 2000) report a method in which the partition is dynamically constructed while the policy is derived. This is a heuristic approach to model reduction, with no guarantees regarding the quality of the approximation or the running time of the process.

Some recently developed examples of these techniques can be found in (Ferns et al, 2006; Barry et al, 2010).

Specialized approaches.

Finally, other approximation techniques have been developed for special kinds of MDPs, or for specialized applications. For example, in (Meuleau et al, 2009) the authors propose a heuristic algorithm for planning with continuous resources, and show its applications to space exploration domains; (Regan and Boutilier, 2010) propose novel techniques for the optimization of MDPs with imprecisely specified rewards.

5.3 BDI and MDP: Bridging the Gap

Finally, we would like to discuss the related work on the topic of combining both approaches to decision making. The idea of using a deterministic planner in the derivation of policies was discussed by the authors in early versions of this work (Simari and Parsons, 2006; Simari, 2004), and is also closely related in spirit to the works of Dean et al (1995); Drummond and Bresina (1990). However, in Dean et al (1995), the authors focus on developing algorithms to compute policies based on a subset of the state space (also called *envelopes*) and subsequently refine this subset to enhance the policy; though the initial envelope may be defined based on a linear plan, the goal is not (as in our work) to come up with a policy that represents this plan, but derive one that is as good as possible using less states. In this sense, our work is more

---

[2] We refer the reader to (Papadimitriou, 1994) for a treatment of the polynomial hierarchy in computational complexity.

closely related to that of Drummond and Bresina (1990), though their work was not in the MDP domain. Similar ideas have subsequently appeared in the autonomous agents and planning literature. For instance, the work of (Gardiol and Kaelbling, 2008) takes a relational description of a planning problem. builds an initial plan, and then produces an *abstract* MDP based on this initial plan, following the approach of Dean et al (1995) described above. The MDP is then refined and expanded iteratively in an anytime fashion. In (Barry et al, 2010), an algorithm is presented for solving large MDPs in a hierarchical manner by first building an abstraction of the state space (as discussed above), and then applying a deterministic approximations to solve the upper levels; the lower levels are treated as small MDPs via conventional algorithms. In the same vein, the approach was also recently adopted in (Teichteil-Konigsbuch et al, 2010); in this work, the authors apply this same basic idea, and further investigate how classical planners can be used to produce policies that are then aggregated incrementally, as well as using Monte Carlo simulations of partial policies in order to assess the probability of having to re-plan during execution. Although the other works mentioned above provide experimental evaluations of their algorithms, this work especially provides empirical validation of this approach; the planning algorithm, called RFF, won the 2008 International Planning Competition (Fully-Observable Probabilistic Planning Track). This clearly supports the feasibility of our theoretical results from Chapter 4 for planning applications. Finally, other signs that the community is moving in this direction can be seen in (Geffner, 2010).

Chapter 6
Conclusions, Limitations, and Future Directions

In this work, we presented empirical data that show that on a particular task there are cases where using an MDP model provides the best solution, while in other cases a BDI approach works best — as the task grows in size beyond the range of problems that can be optimally solved using an MDP, the BDI approach outperforms the best one can do with an MDP. This suggests that some aspects of the BDI approach may be worth considering in more detail. Here we provide some of that detail.

We also presented a novel way of viewing both models of agency, *i.e.*, one in terms of the other. By doing this, we established a series of important relationships between the various components of both models. The results from Section 4.4 show that the BDI model is not inherently sub-optimal. If we can, as the results there show we can in theory, construct a set of intentions that obey an optimal policy, then the BDI model will give us optimal performance. Of course, one of the main features we have been discussing throughout this work is that BDI has the flexibility to construct intentions not necessarily from optimal policies but from domain knowledge; it is because of the mismatch of the two that sub-optimality creeps in. The results in Section 4.4 shed light on the relationship between both models, as they show how BDI plans can be derived from MDP policies, be them optimal or not. Moreover, the results in Section 4.5 can also help us in practice, as they show us how to construct policies from *i*-plans; this means that we can create *i*-plans in situations where the state-space is so large that it is not possible to generate anything like an optimal policy. As discussed above, work developed in the last few years has shown that this approach is feasible and could lead to faster and better planners for complex stochastic domains.

6.1 Limitations

As mentioned in Section 3.4, the main limitation of our empirical evaluation lies in the fact that state-of-the-art approximations and implementations were not used; however, our goal was not to evaluate specific techniques and algorithms, but to investigate key aspects of the two models. It is important to note that the results obtained regarding these key aspects hold despite the basic nature of our approximation algorithms. Regarding our theoretical study, the discussion in Section 4.4.2 suggests that we can use the relationships we have developed to construct policies at a sufficiently abstract level that we can gain some computational advantage over directly solving an MDP. Though we have demonstrated that it is possible to do this in theory, one of the limitations of this work is that we have not done so in practice. However, as we mentioned in Chapter 5, some work towards this end has already started to surface in the literature.

6.2 Future Work

Future work in this research line will be dedicated to drawing further conclusions from the initial results that were obtained in this work.

We are currently focusing on deriving algorithms that effectively map BDI specifications into MDP specifications (and *vice versa*), and obtaining both empirical and theoretical validations of these mappings. It would be interesting to compare the results we obtain with those obtained in the increasingly more applied approaches that are being developed in the literature, as discussed in Chapter 5; it is possible that our "big picture" approach may lead to an even deeper understanding of the relationship between the two models that we have been concerned with in this work.

References

Albore A, Palacios H, Geffner H (2009) A translation-based approach to contingent planning. In: Proceedings of the 21st international joint conference on Artifical intelligence, Morgan Kaufmann Publishers Inc., San Francisco, CA, USA, pp 1623–1628

Barry J, Kaelbling LP, Lozano-perez T (2010) Hierarchical solution of large Markov Decision Processes. In: Proceedings of ICAPS 2010 Workshop on Planning and Scheduling Under Uncertainty

Bellman R (1957) A Markovian decision process. Journal of Mathematics and Mechanics 6

Boutilier C, Dean T, Hanks S (1999) Decision-theoretic planning: Structural assumptions and computational leverage. Journal of Artificial Intelligence Research 11:1–94

Boutilier C, Dearden R, Goldszmidt M (2000) Stochastic dynamic programming with factored representations. Artificial Intelligence 121(1–2):49–107

Bratman ME (1987) Intentions, Plans, and Practical Reason. Harvard University Press, Cambridge, Massachusetts, U.S.A.

Bratman ME (1990) What is intention? In: Cohen, Morgan and Pollack, eds. Intentions in Communication, MIT Press

Bratman ME, Israel D, Pollack ME (1991) Plans and resource-bounded practical reasoning. In: Cummins R, Pollock JL (eds) Philosophy and AI: Essays at the Interface, The MIT Press, Cambridge, Massachusetts, pp 1–22

Burmeister B, Arnold M, Copaciu F, Rimassa G (2008) BDI-agents for agile goal-oriented business processes. In: Proceedings of AAMAS 2008 (Industry Track, IFAAMAS, Richland, SC, AAMAS '08, pp 37–44

Busetta P, Ronnquist R, Hodgson A, Lucas A (1999) JACK intelligent agents — components for intelligent agents in Java. White Paper, Agent Oriented Software Group

Clarke EM, Jha S, Lu Y, Wang D (1999) Abstract bdds: A technque for using abstraction in model checking. In: Proceedings of CHARME 1999, Springer-Verlag, London, UK, CHARME '99, pp 172–186

Cohen PR, Levesque HJ (1990) Intention is choice with commitment. Artificial Intelligence 42:213–261

De Giacomo G, Patrizi F, Sardiña S (2010) Agent programming via planning programs. In: Proceedings of AAMAS 2010, IFAAMAS, Richland, SC, AAMAS '10, pp 491–498

Dean T, Boddy M (1988) An analysis of time-dependent planning. In: Proceedings of AAAI 1988, AAAI Press, pp 49–54

Dean T, Kaelbling LP, Kirman J, Nicholson A (1995) Planning under time constraints in stochastic domains. Artificial Intelligence 76(1-2):35 – 74, planning and Scheduling

Dean T, Givan R, Leach S (1997) Model reduction techniques for computing approximately optimal solutions for Markov decision processes. In: Proceedings of UAI 1997, Providence, RI, pp 124–131

Debenham J, Sierra C (2010) Dual rationality and deliberative agents. In: Bramer M, Ellis R, Petridis M (eds) Research and Development in Intelligent Systems XXVI, Springer London, pp 79–92

D'Inverno M, Luck M, Georgeff M, Kinny D, Wooldridge M (July 2004) The dMARS architecture: A specification of the distributed multi-agent reasoning system. Autonomous Agents and Multi-Agent Systems 9:5–53(49)

Drummond M, Bresina JL (1990) Anytime synthetic projection: Maximizing the probability of goal satisfaction. In: Proceedings of AAAI 1990, pp 138–144

Eiter T, Subrahmanian VS, Pick G (1999) Heterogeneous active agents, I: semantics. Artificial Intelligence 108:179–255

Errecalde ML (2003) Aprendizaje basado en múltiples fuentes de experiencia. PhD thesis, Universidad Nacional del Sur, Bahía Blanca, Argentina

Fagundes M, Vicari R, Coelho H (2009) Deliberation process in a BDI model with Bayesian networks. In: Ghose A, Governatori G, Sadananda R (eds) Agent Computing and Multi-Agent Systems, LNCS, vol 5044, Springer Berlin / Heidelberg, pp 207–218

Ferns N, Castro P, Precup D, Panangaden P (2006) Methods for computing state similarity in Markov Decision Processes. In: Proceedings of UAI 2006, AUAI Press, Arlington, Virginia, pp 174–181

Fisher M (1997) Implementing BDI-like systems by direct execution. In: Proceedings of IJCAI 1997, pp 316–321

Gardiol NH, Kaelbling LP (2008) Adaptive envelope MDPs for relational equivalence-based planning. Tech. Rep. MIT-CSAIL-TR-2008-050, MIT CS & AI Lab, Cambridge, MA

Geffner H (2010) The model-based approach to autonomous behavior: A personal view. In: Proceedings of AAAI 2010

Georgeff MP, Ingrand FF (1989) Decision-making in embedded reasoning systems. In: Proceedings of IJCAI 1989, Detroit, MI, pp 972–978

Goldman RP, Musliner DJ, Durfee EH (2009) Coordinating highly contingent plans: Biasing distributed mdps towards cooperative behavior. In: ICAPS 2008 Multiagent Planning Workshop

Goldsmith J, Sloan RH (2000) The complexity of model aggregation. In: Proceedings of the 5th Interrnational Conference on Artificial Intelligence Planning and Scheduling Systems, Breckenridge, CO, pp 122–129

Hermanns H, Wachter B, Zhang L (2008) Probabilistic CEGAR. In: Proceedings of CAV 2008, Springer-Verlag, Berlin, Heidelberg, CAV '08, pp 162–175

Howden N, Ronnquist R, Hodgson A, Lucas A (2001) JACK intelligent agents — summary of an agent infrastructure. In: Proceedings of the 5th International Conference on Autonomous Agents, Montreal

Huber MJ (1999) JAM: a BDI-theoretic mobile agent architecture. In: Proceedings of the Third International Conference on Autonomous Agents, Seattle, Washington, pp 236–243

Jo CH, Arnold AJ (2002) The agent-based programming language: APL. In: Proceedings of ACM SAC 2002, Madrid, Spain, pp 27–31

Kattenbelt M, Kwiatkowska M, Norman G, Parker D (2010) A game-based abstraction-refinement framework for Markov Decision Processes. Formal Methods in System Design 36:246–280

Kinny DN, Georgeff MP (1991) Commitment and effectiveness of situated agents. In: Proceedings of IJCAI 1991, Sydney, Australia, pp 82–88

Kwiatkowska M, Norman G, Parker D (2010) Advances and challenges of probabilistic model checking. In: Proceedings of the 48th Annual Allerton Conference on Communication, Control and Computing

Littman ML (1996) Algorithms for sequential decision making. PhD thesis, Department of Computer Science, Brown University, Providence, RI

Lovejoy WS (1991) A survey of algorithmic methods for partially observable Markov decision processes. Annals of Operations Research 28(1):47–65

Machado R, Bordini R (2002) Running AgentSpeak(L) agents on SIM_AGENT. In: Meyer JJ, Tambe M (eds) Intelligent Agents VIII, LNCS, vol 2333, Springer Verlag, Berlin, pp 158–174

Mataríc MJ (1994) Reward functions for accelerated learning. In: Proceedings of ICML 1994, New Brunswick, NJ, pp 181–189

Meneguzzi FR, Zorzo AF, da Costa Móra M (2004) Propositional planning in BDI agents. In: Proceedings of ACM SAC 2004, ACM, New York, NY, USA, SAC '04, pp 58–63

Meuleau N, Benazera E, Brafman RI, Hansen EA, Mausam M (2009) A heuristic search approach to planning with continuous resources in stochastic domains. Journal of Artificial Intelligence Research 34:27–59

Papadimitriou CH (1994) Computatational Complexity. Addison-Wesley, Reading, Mass.

Parsons S, Pettersson O, Saffiotti A, Wooldridge M (1999) Robots with the best of intentions. In: Proceedings of Towards Intelligent Mobile Robots 99, Manchester, UK

Pollack ME, Ringuette M (1990) Introducing the Tileworld: experimentally evaluating agent architectures. In: Proceedings of AAAI 1990, Boston, MA, pp 183–189

Puterman ML (1994) Markov Decision Processes: Discrete Stochastic Dynamic Programming. John Wiley and Sons, Inc., New York

Raiffa H (1968) Decision Analysis: Introductory Lectures on Choices under Uncertainty. Addison-Wesley

Rao AS, Georgeff MP (1991) Deliberation and its role in the formation of intentions. In: Proceedings of UAI 1991, Los Angeles, CA, pp 300–307

Rao AS, Georgeff MP (1995) BDI-agents: from theory to practice. In: Proceedings of the 1st International Conference on Multiagent Systems, San Francisco, CA

Regan K, Boutilier C (2010) Robust policy computation in reward-uncertain MDPs using nondominated policies. In: Proceedings of AAAI 2010

Russell S, Wefald E (1992) Do the right thing: Studies in limited rationality. MIT press

Russell SJ, Subramanian D, Parr R (1993) Provably bounded optimal agents. In: Proceedings of the 13th International Joint Conference on Artificial Intelligence, Chambéry, France, pp 338–344

Sardiña S, de Silva L, Padgham L (2006) Hierarchical planning in BDI agent programming languages: a formal approach. In: Proceedings of AAMAS 2006, ACM, New York, NY, USA, AAMAS '06, pp 1001–1008

Schoppers MJ (1987) Universal plans for reactive robots in unpredictable environments. In: Proceedings of IJCAI 1987, Milan, Italy, pp 1039–1046

Schut M, Wooldridge M (2000) Intention reconsideration in complex environments. In: Proceedings of the 4th International Conference on Autonomous Agents, Barcelona, Spain, pp 209–216

Schut M, Wooldridge M (2001) Principles of intention reconsideration. In: Proceedings of the 5th International Conference on Autonomous Agents, Montreal, Canada, pp 340–347

Schut M, Wooldridge M, Parsons S (2001) Reasoning about intentions in uncertain domains. In: Proceedings of ECSQARU 2001, Toulouse, France, pp 84–95

Schut M, Wooldridge M, Parsons S (2004) The theory and practice of intention reconsideration. Journal of Theoretical and Experimental AI 16(4):261–293

Schut MC (2002) Intention reconsideration. PhD thesis, University of Liverpool

Sierhuis M, Clancey WJ, van Hoof RJ, Seah CH, Scott MS, Nado RA, Blumenberg SF, Shafto MG, Anderson BL, Bruins AC, Buckley CB, Diegelman TE, Hall TA, Hood D, Reynolds FF, Toschlog JR, Tucker T (2009) Nasa's OCA mirroring system: An application of multiagent systems in mission control. In: Proceedings of AAMAS 2009 (Industry Track), IFAAMAS, pp 85–92

Simari GI (2004) Rational decision making in autonomous agents. Master's thesis, Universidad Nacional del Sur, Bahía Blanca, Argentina

Simari GI, Parsons S (2006) On the relationship between MDPs and the BDI architecture. In: Proceedings of AAMAS 2006, ACM Press, New York, NY, pp 1041–1048

Stroe B, Subrahmanian V, Dasgupta S (2005) Optimal status sets of heterogeneous agent programs. In: Proceedings of AAMAS 2005, ACM, New York, NY, USA, AAMAS '05, pp 709–715

Sutton RS, Barto AG (1998) Reinforcement Learning: An Introduction. MIT Press, Cambridge, MA

Tan AH, Feng YH, Ong YS (2010) A self-organizing neural architecture integrating desire, intention and reinforcement learning. Neurocomputing 73:1465–1477

Teichteil-Konigsbuch F, Kuter U, Infantes G (2010) Incremental plan aggregation for generating policies in MDPs. In: Proceedings AAMAS 2010, IFAAMAS, pp 1231–1238

Thrun S, Fox D, Burgard W, Dellaert F (2001) Robust Monte Carlo localization for mobile robots. Artificial Intelligence 128(1–2):99–141

Trigo P, Coelho H (2008) A hybrid approach to multi-agent decision-making. In: Proceeding of ECAI 2008, IOS Press, Amsterdam, The Netherlands, pp 413–417

Tsitsiklis J, van Roy B (1996) Feature-based methods for large scale dynamic programming. Machine Learning 22(1/2/3):59–94

Winikoff M (2005) JACK intelligent agents: An industrial strength platform. In: Weiss G, Bordini R, Dastani M, Dix J, Fallah Seghrouchni A (eds) Multi-Agent Programming, Multiagent Systems, Artificial Societies, and Simulated Organizations, vol 15, Springer US, pp 175–193

Wooldridge M (1999) Intelligent Agents. In: Weiss G (ed) Multiagent Systems - A Modern Approach to Distributed Artificial Intelligence, The MIT Press, Cambridge, Massachussetts, pp 27–78

Wooldridge M (2000) Reasoning about Rational Agents. The MIT Press: Cambridge, MA, USA

Wooldridge M, Parsons S (1999) Intention reconsideration reconsidered. In: Müller J, Singh MP, Rao AS (eds) Intelligent Agents V, Springer-Verlag, Heidelberg, Germany, LNAI, vol 1555, pp 63–80

Index